High Shelf

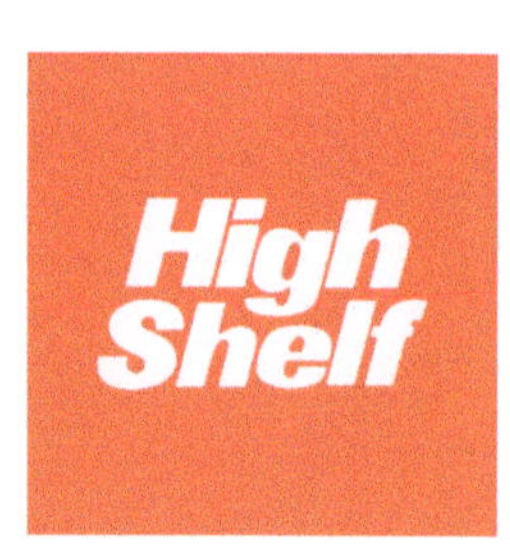

High Shelf Issue XIII, December 2019
Portland, Oregon.
Copyright 2019, High Shelf Press

ISBN: 978-1-7342842-1-8

Cover Image by Ja Min Yie
Design and Layout by C. M. Tollefson
Edited by David Seung & C. M. Tollefson

High Shelf XIII

"...somehow
I have always known
anticipated, missed, and dreaded
the same fate
seeking a refuge
in the night sky
and in wild flowers"

Alicja Kusiak-Brownstein

"...Stars need vast emptiness to exist—

you can't get close enough to hear their roar."

Holly Woodward

Table Of Contents

Cathexis

M Zaman

Poetry or not, vagaries of life will still feel
prickly; love or no love, things-that-matter
will still be overwhelming; God or no God,
life's journey will still be a perilous journey.

This is not about the aboutness of myself
or of my poetry or of anything else under
the folds of heathen Gods. Neither celestial
nor interstellar; it's the obelisk of hope.

Neither Calliope nor Erato is my forte; not
even Sappho, the tenth. I do not write for
posterity or for some transcendent euphemism.

When the mind is fenestrated through and
through, when ennui engulfs the total being
like a shroud of death, poetry seeps in;

Butea (Flame of Forest) blooms and sets this
sinking heart ablaze.

Poet's practice

Nan Williamson

There was a time when you wrote
that autumn dazzled   struck our maple trees
and they were rich   deep red and golden leaves
You said that early sunsets left them burning
hectic just before the night

This year   headlines speak of *Nightmares*
The House of Smoke and Mirrors   Dark Rentals
of the Soul   Foul Play   Conduct Unbecoming
Bosses Behaving Badly   a Machiavelli Multi-
Masked who can Smile and Smile and Be a Villain

Outside   there are sirens   someone's been shot

Now   you write   that trees are sick
pathetic fallacy leaves wrinkled   crispy
brown   shrivelled on the branch   Falling
into dusty piles when weak and withered
they break from dried-out stems

Listen   you must still speak of the shadowy
woman who hums silky blue tunes by the night
window   of violets dappling the lawn   of lovers
who somehow survive   and once again   without irony
offer to the betrayed world   one persistent
green shoot that springs from a spent maple tree

The Thoughts of Trees
Briana Gervat

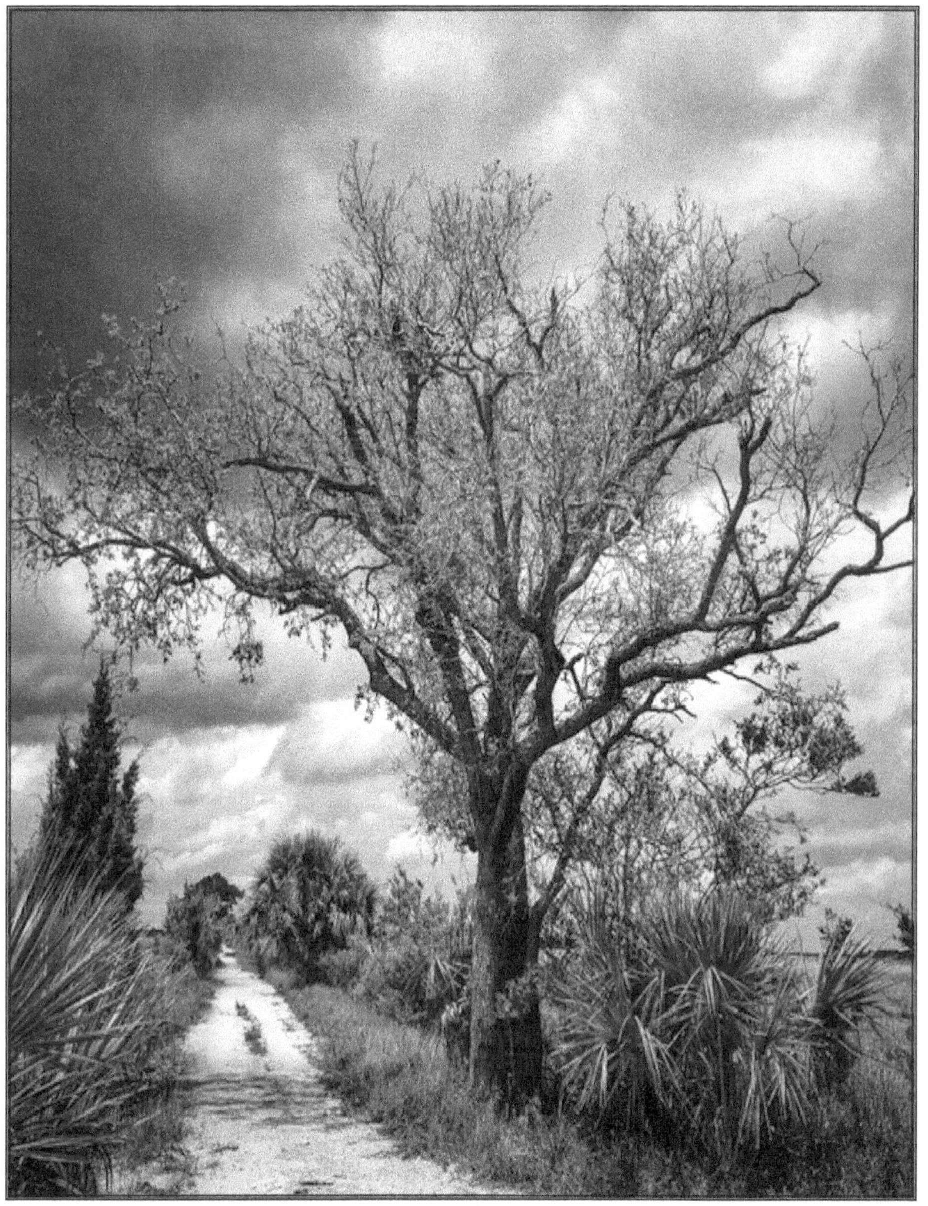

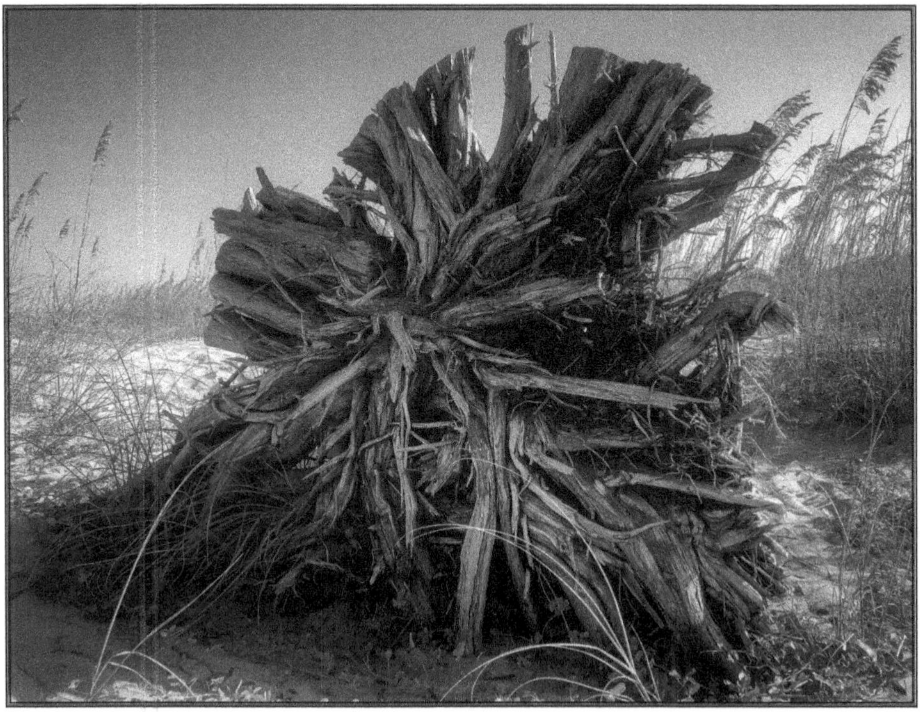

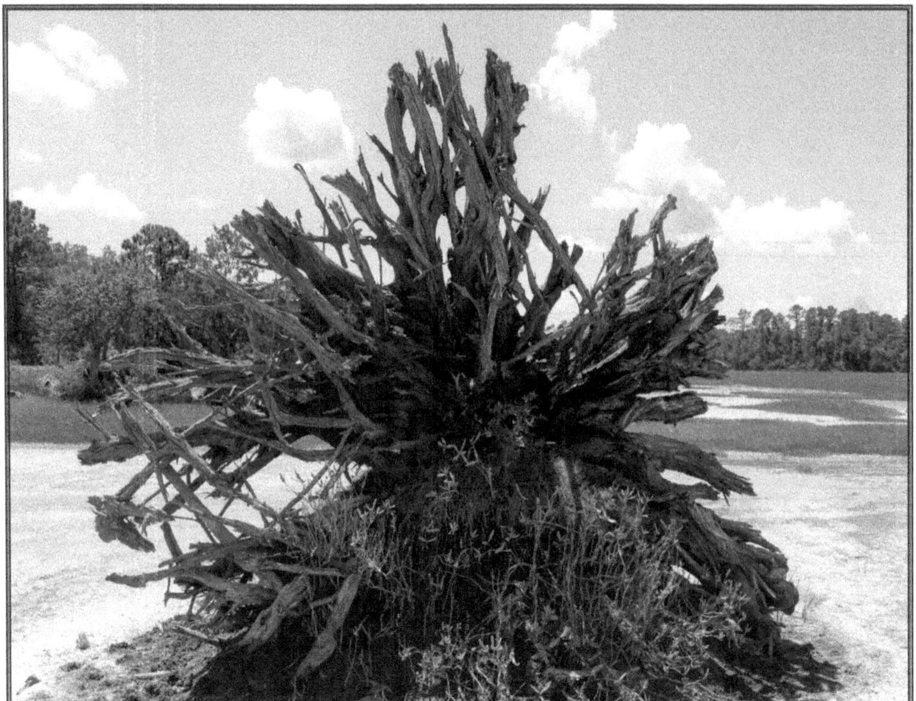

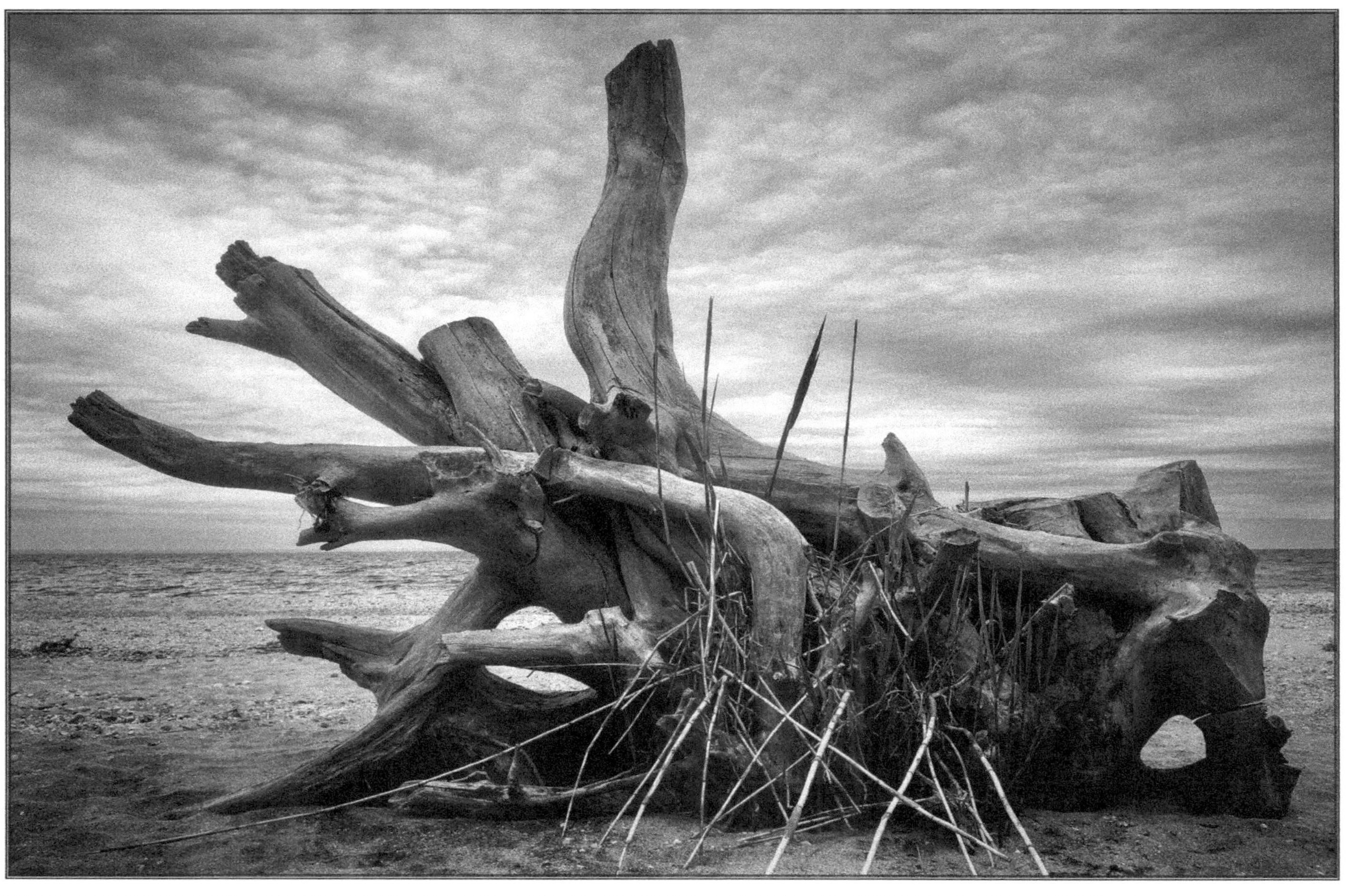

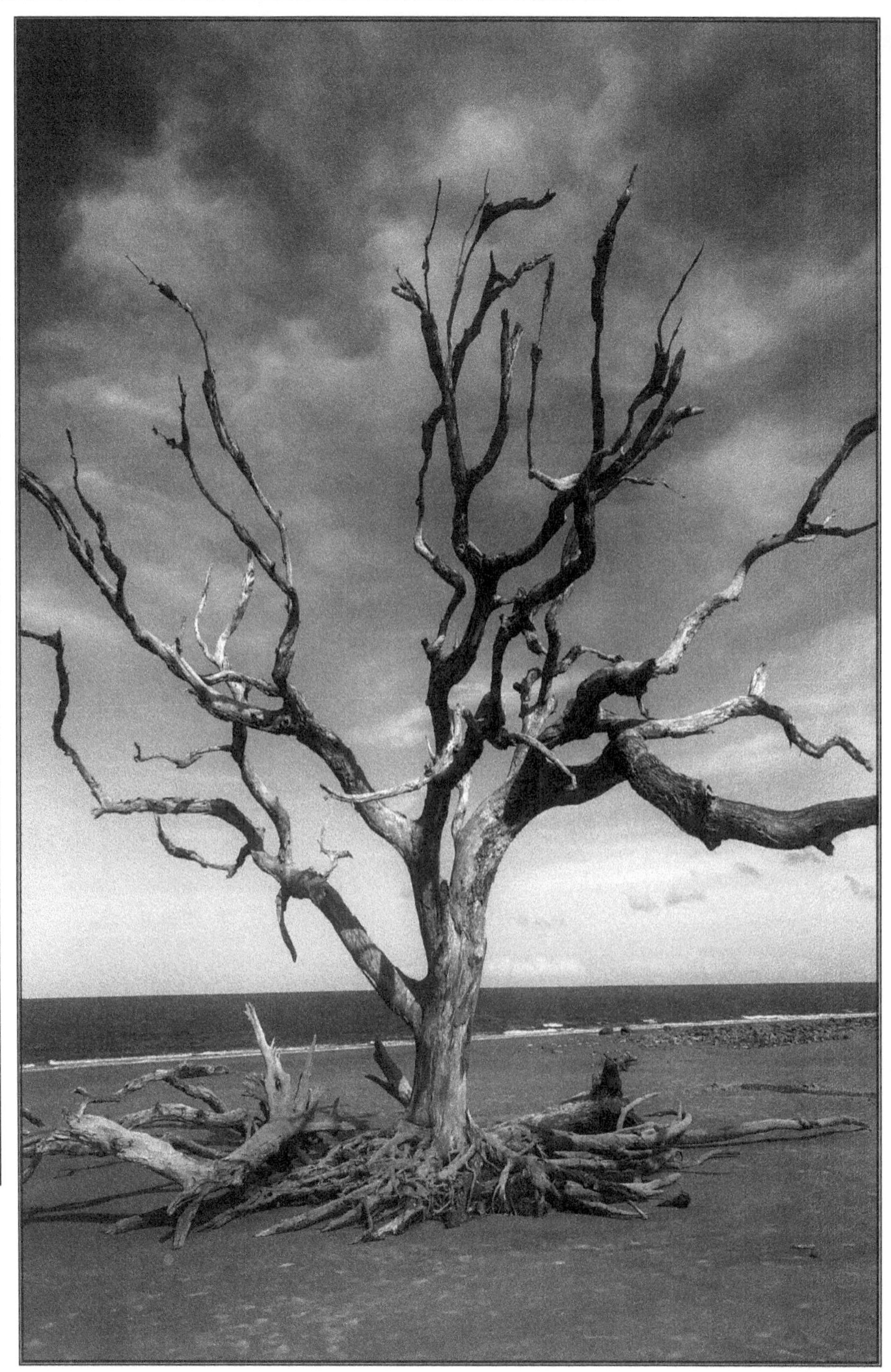

postmemory

Alicja Kusiak-Brownstein

somehow
I have always known
what had happened here

maybe I overheard it
in my mother's womb

maybe she overheard it
in her mother's womb

and her own womb
whispered to me
what had happened here

this place is my womb
as it used to be theirs

I have fed on their bones
and dreams
reluctantly and insatiably
a blessed curse
a cursed blessing

somehow
I have always known
that I should seek out their presence
in the night sky
rather than in muddy soil

somehow
I have always known
that I should sense their presence
in wild flowers
rather than in their crumbling possessions

those who walked my paths
whose eyes turned into sand
whose fingers turned into tree roots
whose voices linger in my dreams
whose dreams linger in my memory
once

gazed at the same sky
and touched the same wild flowers

somehow
I have always known
anticipated, missed, and dreaded
the same fate
seeking a refuge
in the night sky
and in wild flowers

waiting at a café
Katherine Russell

macaron like a kiss, your
pillow pair of lips, like
a sweet ditty from a finch
on the sill, the music
that writes itself
in our world: the off-rhythm
of natural rhythm, the terrible
timing of everything,
like car horns in rainstorms
ripping through the quiet South,
where the heat
opens its mouth
to catch us like swill.

what will we do
to rid a fever with an ice cube,
a hard swallow, a forgetting
again and again—

did chaos make our timing,
or did time make the chaos?
maybe we were supposed to meet
at 4 o'clock another decade,
not a few years after my wedding, not
before i'd given up or during indecision; now,
here's a cookie to remember hunger
and the icing is thinning
so hurry, hurry into the rain rhythm;
our sins depend on it

because the sugar is melting
off our plate whether or not
you care how delicate
joy is, how perfect it tastes
when it first meets our tongues.

Ivory

Abby Conrad

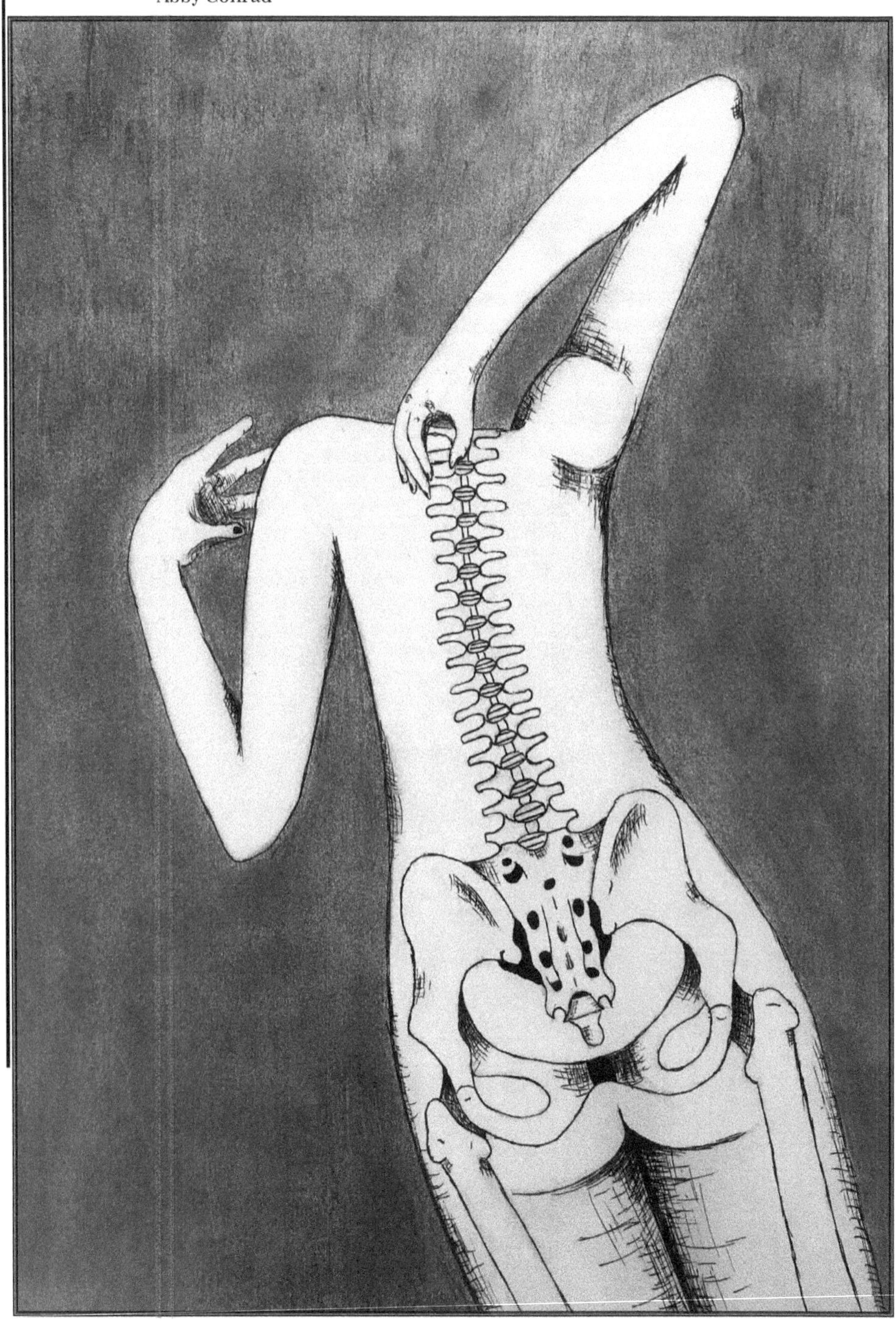

Sex with a Poem

River E. Hall

each comma comes
in depth of cleavage
cut of hipbone

pulsating dashes inside:
parenthesis of open mouths holding
(salivary-sounds) enjambed between legs

some demand strange geometry:
sharp angles against round of cranium
(skull-fuckery) commanding submission
to right angles of the page

a poem enters a poem from behind
discordant tenses tensing around the girth

some are stranger sex:
shallow dialogues until they
whisper salt water in the ear
(voices muffled) until poured out
a warm stain on a pillowcase

some are rough:
fucking through the sternum
slithering between ribs
pressing up through the breasts

some are quick:
find quiet places in ventricles
to go limp
sleep

leaving the poet staring at the ceiling

I'm so fucking bored

Michal Vojtech

I cannonballed into my bath tub
swam front crawl
until all the water splashed out

I sat down on the toilet
listened to my breath

stood at the mirror
touched up my make up

mentally prepared
to fuck myself

in all the corners of the apartment
and leave in the morning without
saying goodbye

Debt Collectors, Heartache and Camisoles

Kathleen Tryon

Again, empty bowl. Again,
thirst. This time,
tornados over Missouri.

And again, a city shatters.
Now, I'm flood water at your door
balancing fallen brick

on the tip of my tongue. Chin
jacked up. I can't stop
looking up

words for lost love.
Black, red, bruised
lip biting, frozen, dark

chocolate. Spattered
coffee on yellow walls. Brown tears.
The whole damn scene's so soggy.

For the life of me
I can't remember how to scatter
showers, clear sky, save a lilac's aroma

from wilting. So I slip
silky garments under my blouse
to appear smooth

I have a drawer full
shear and see through.
Half started, ripped up

apology notes I owe you. Red
rings round blue eyes. We stare
out the window. Both smoke.

You hook a leash to the neck
of our limping old dog.
Flies buzz by. Branches quiver.

Worms float dead in puddles.
I bend first. Again,
we rake through rubble.

Transitory Space, Circle Rocks, Nova Scotia, Canada
Leah Oates

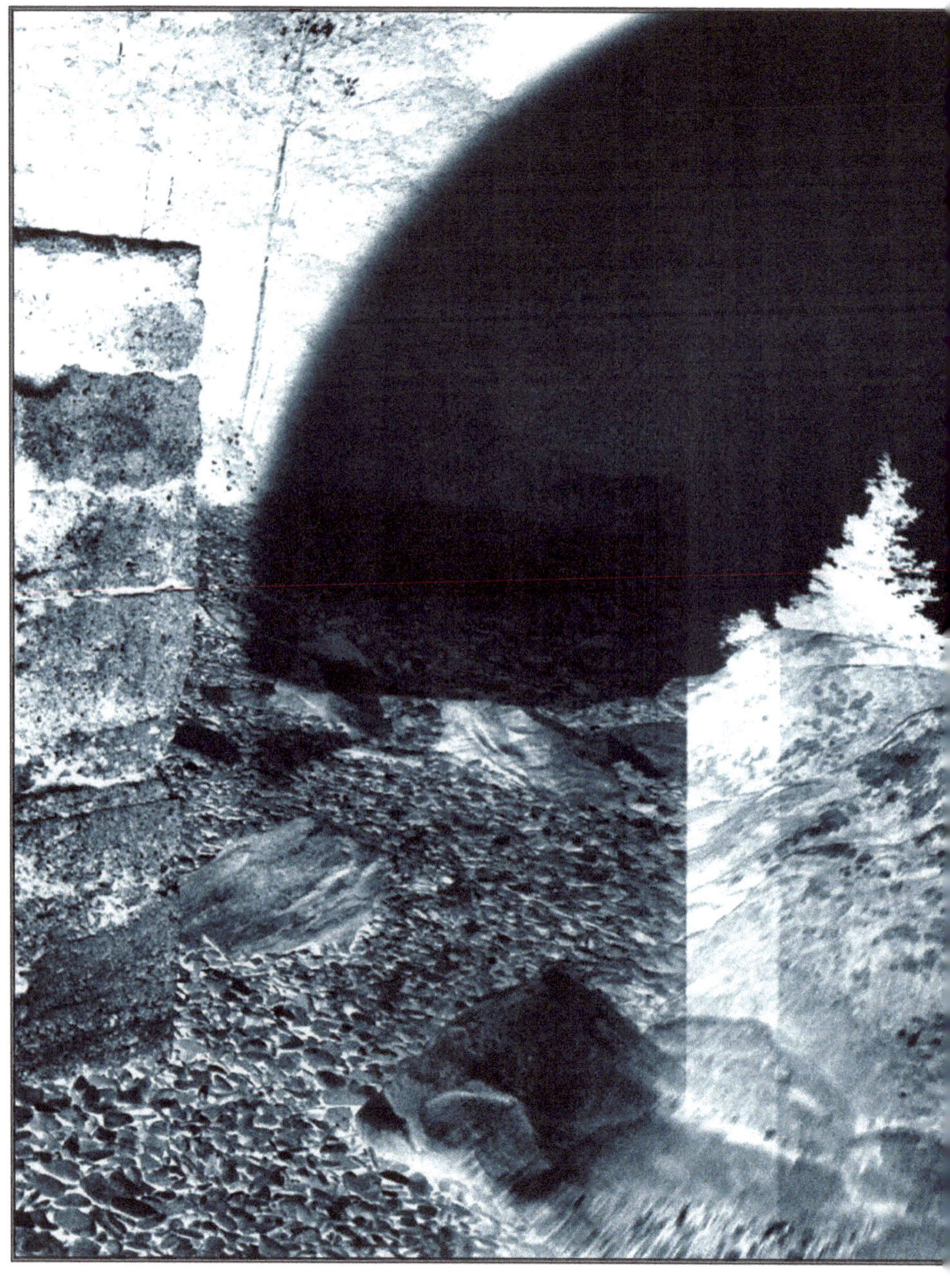

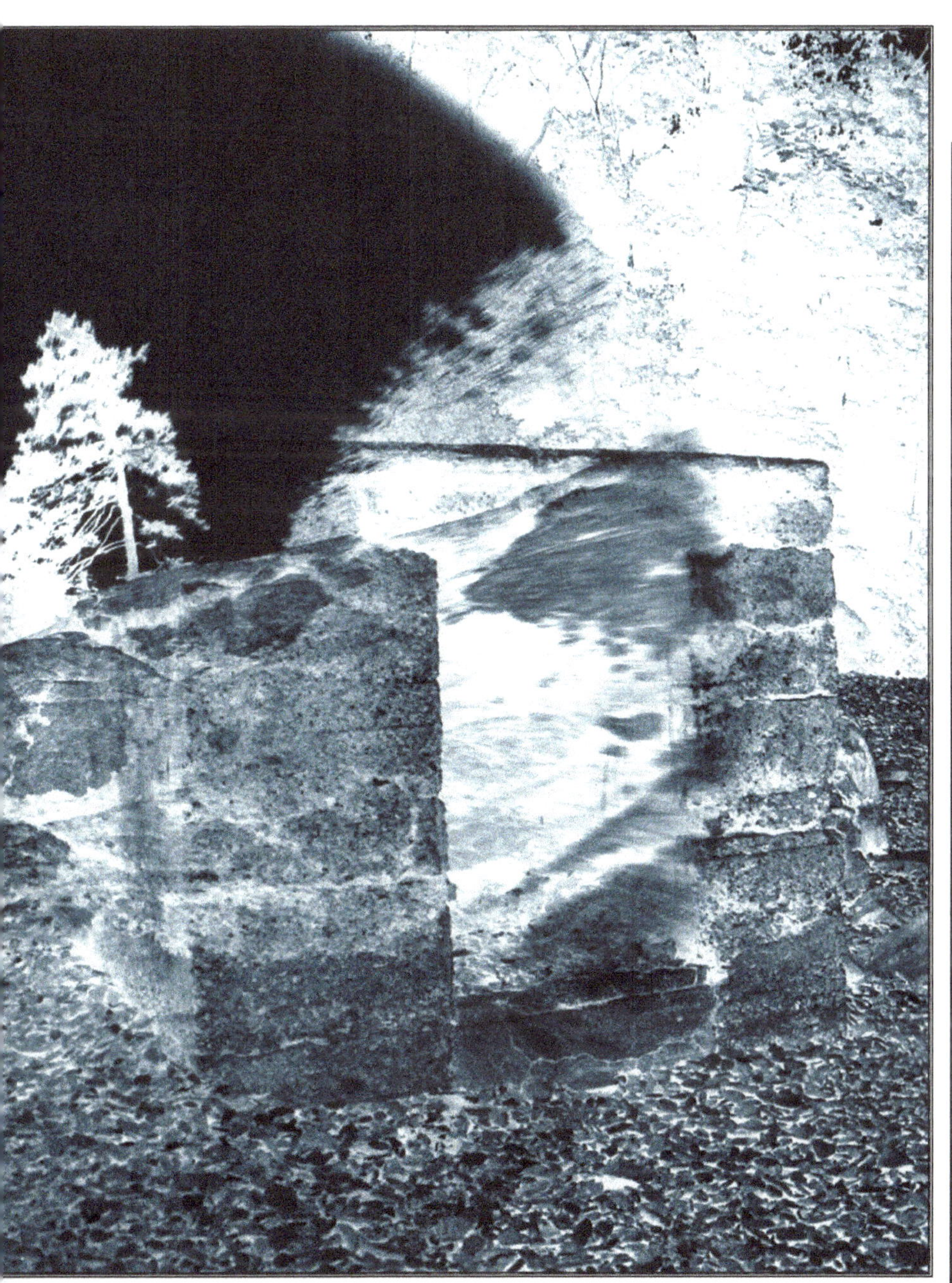

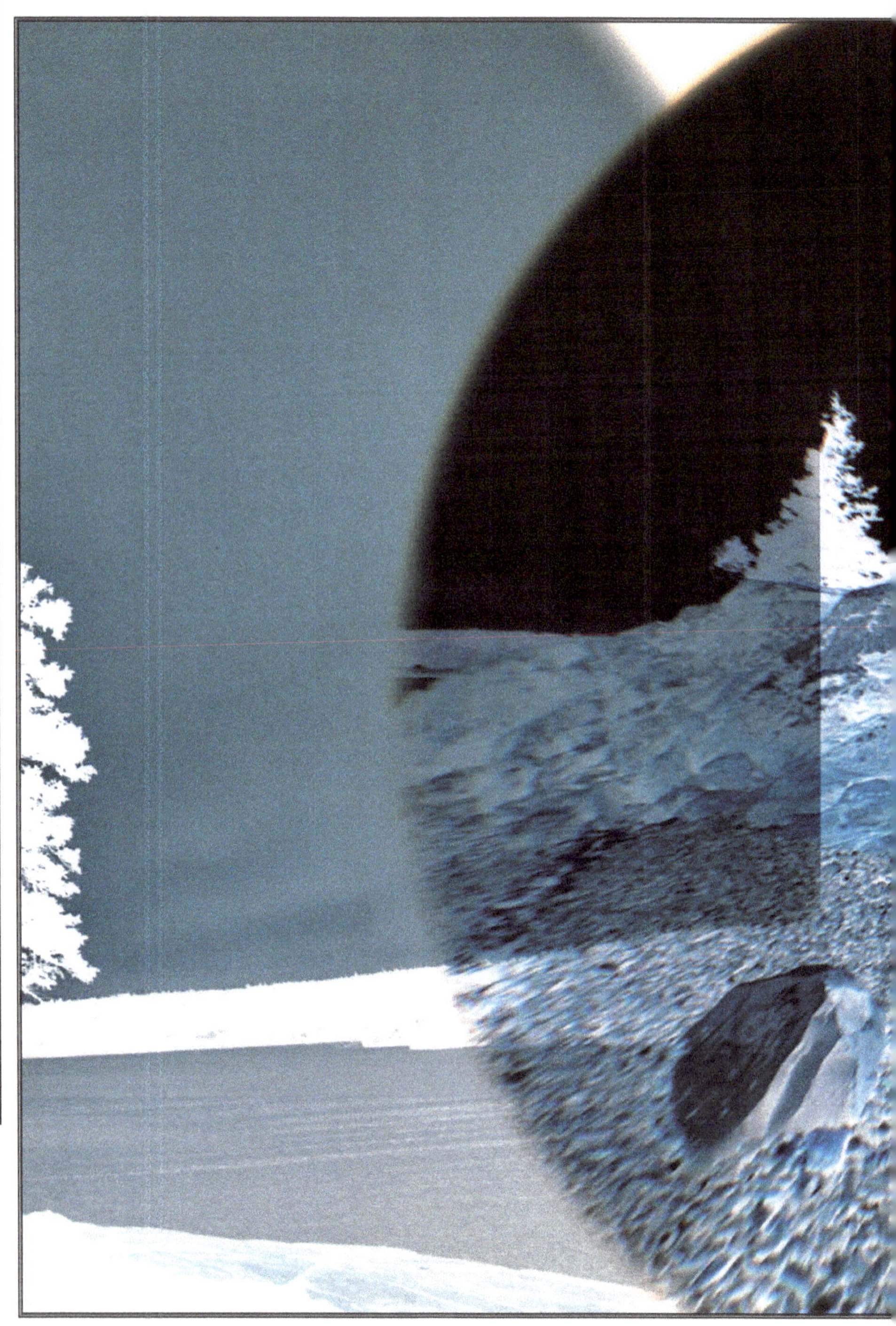

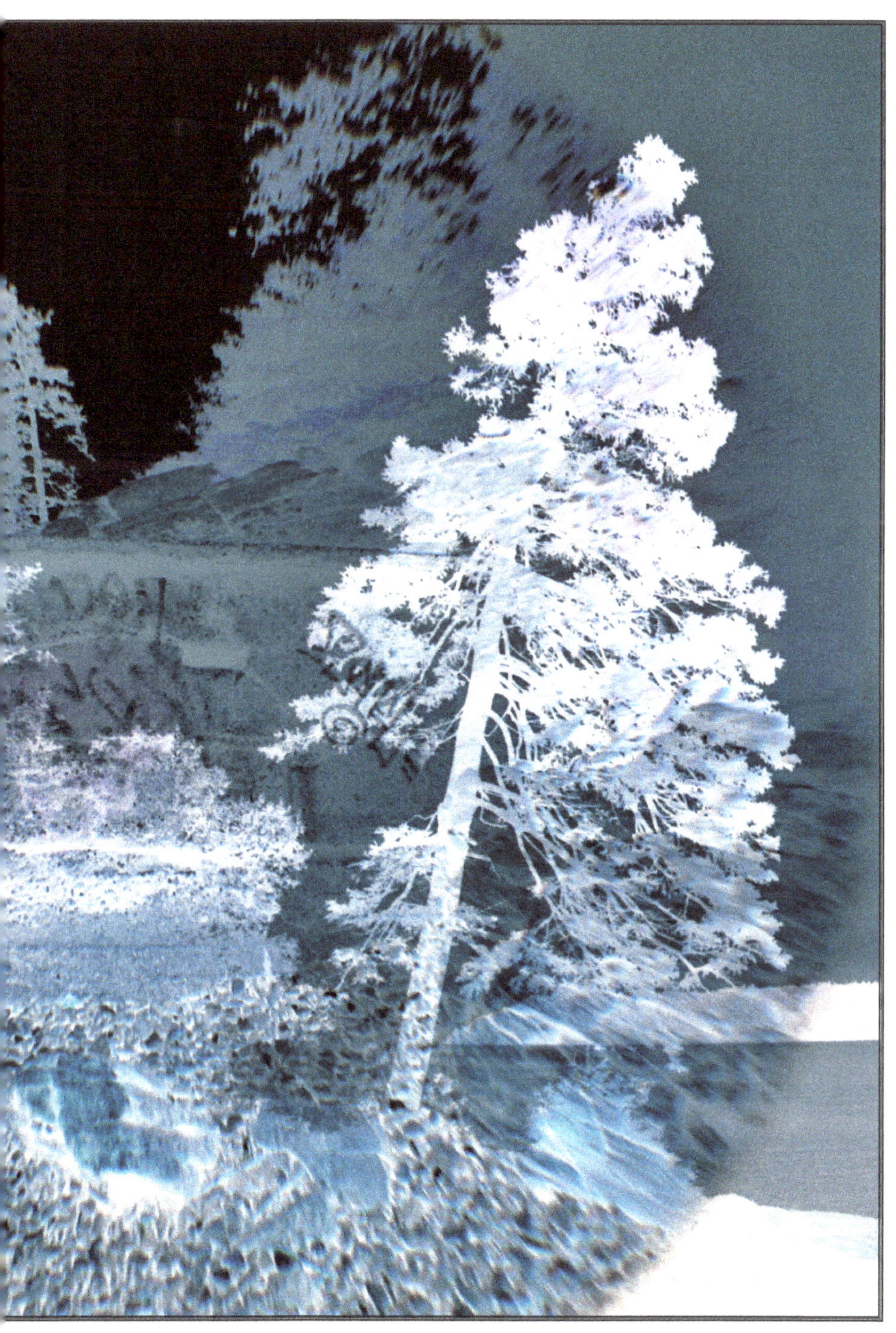

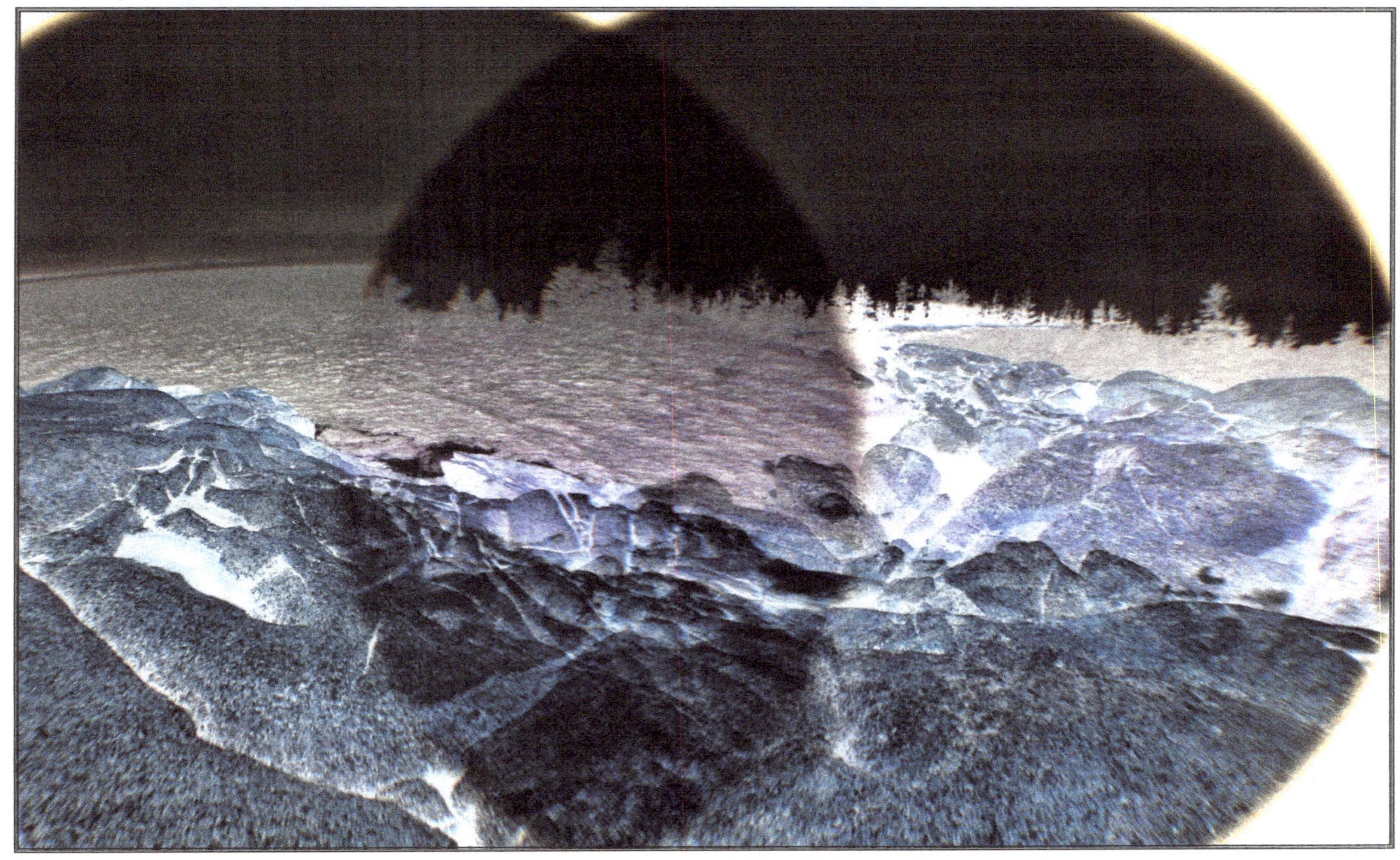

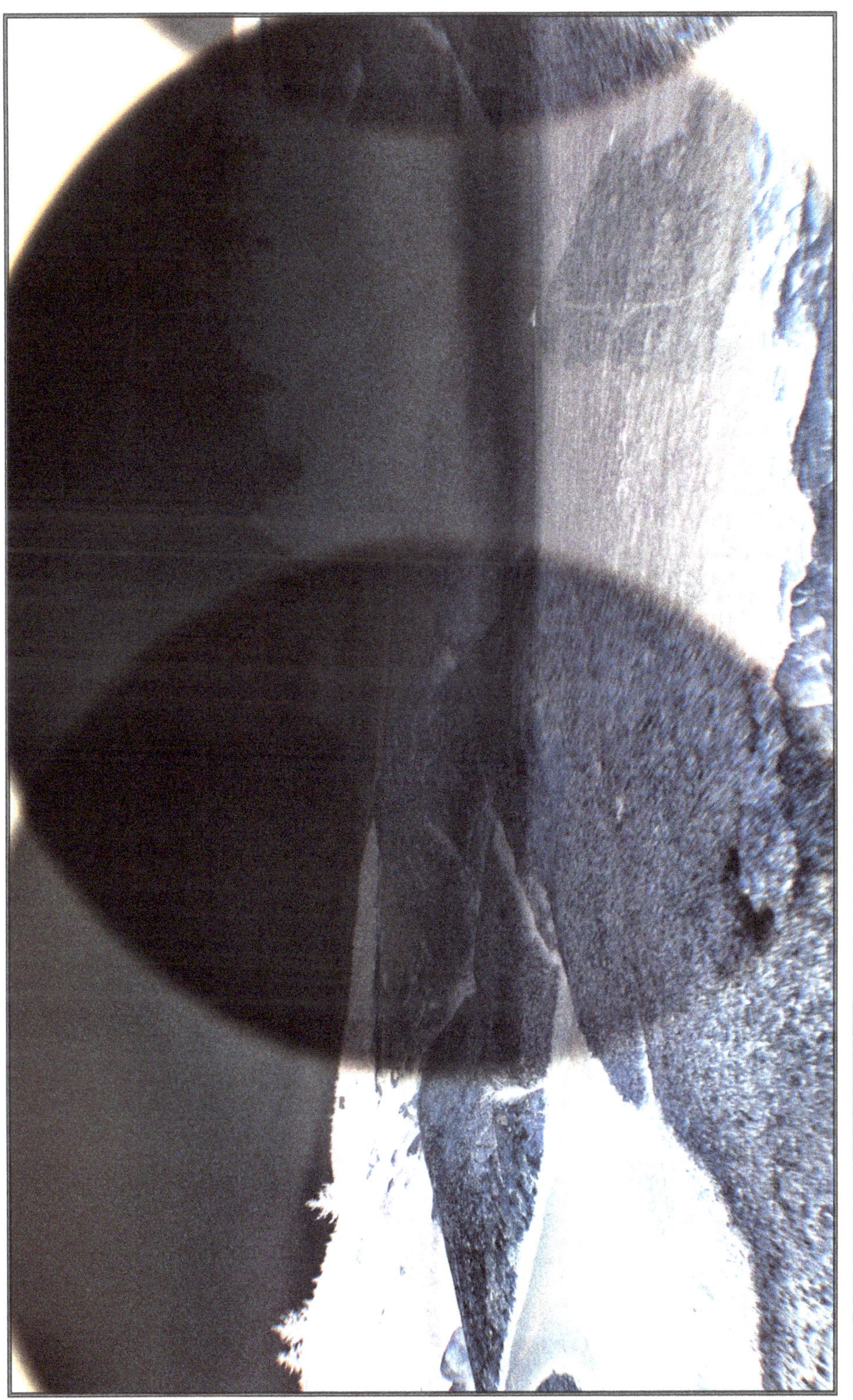

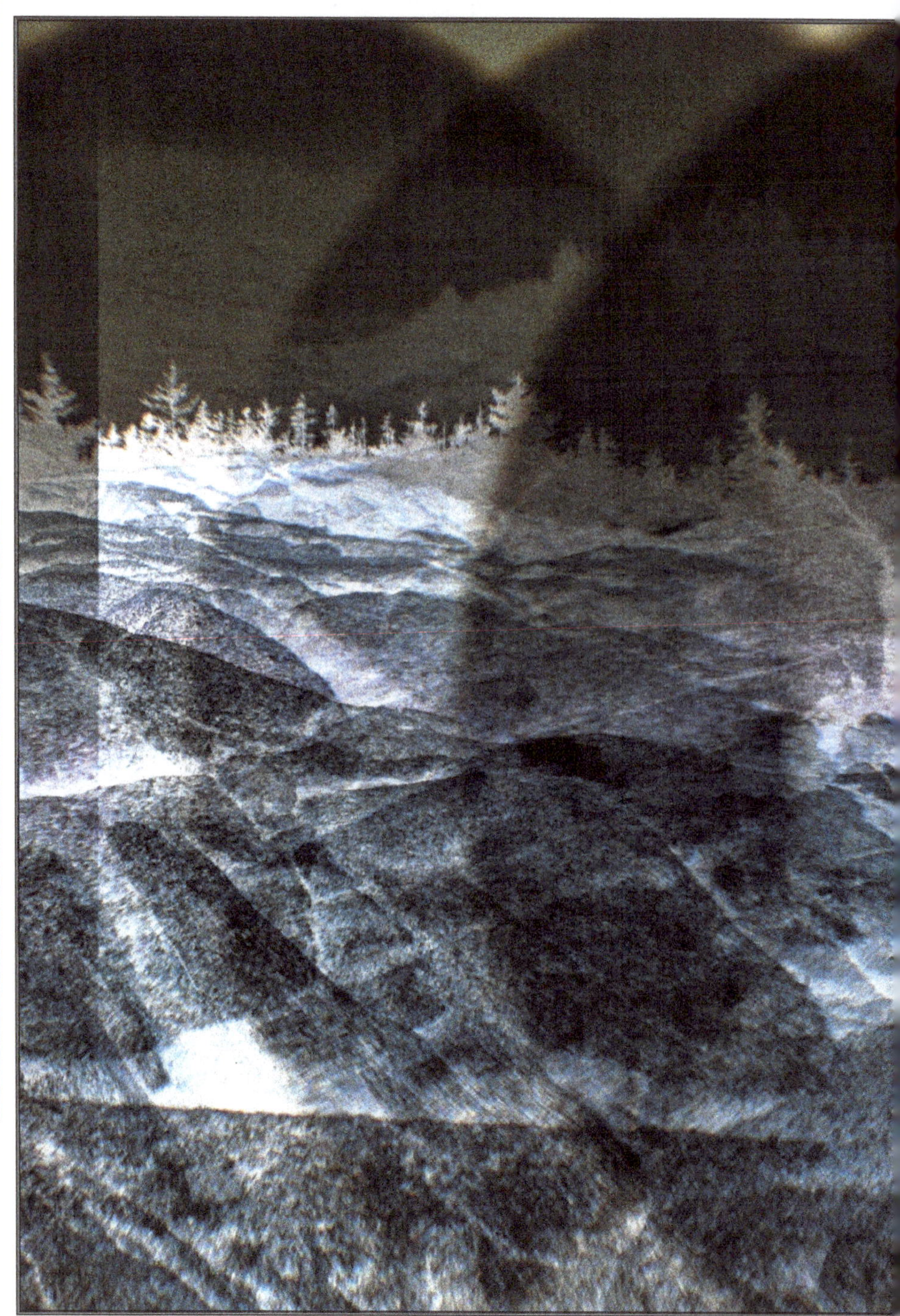

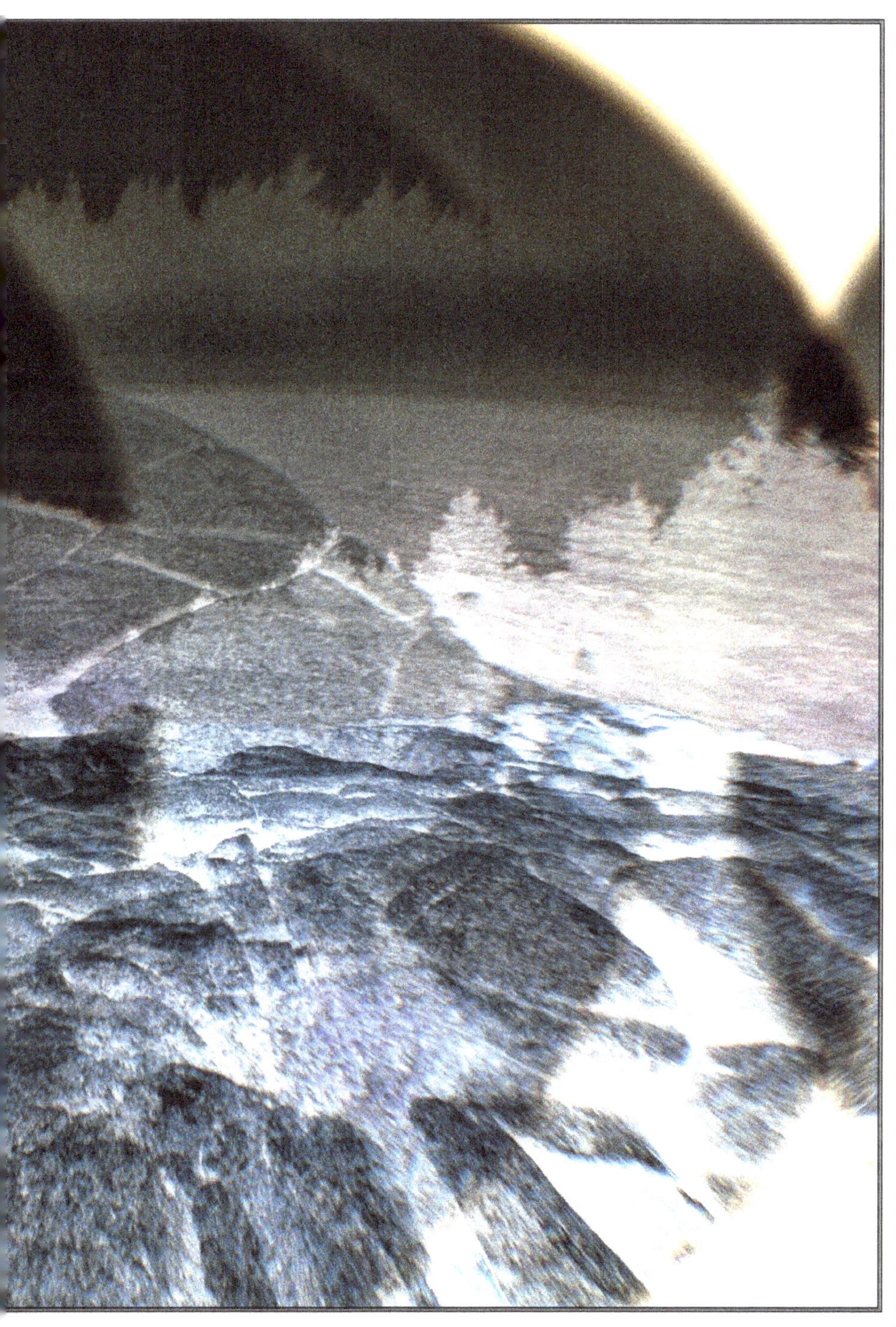

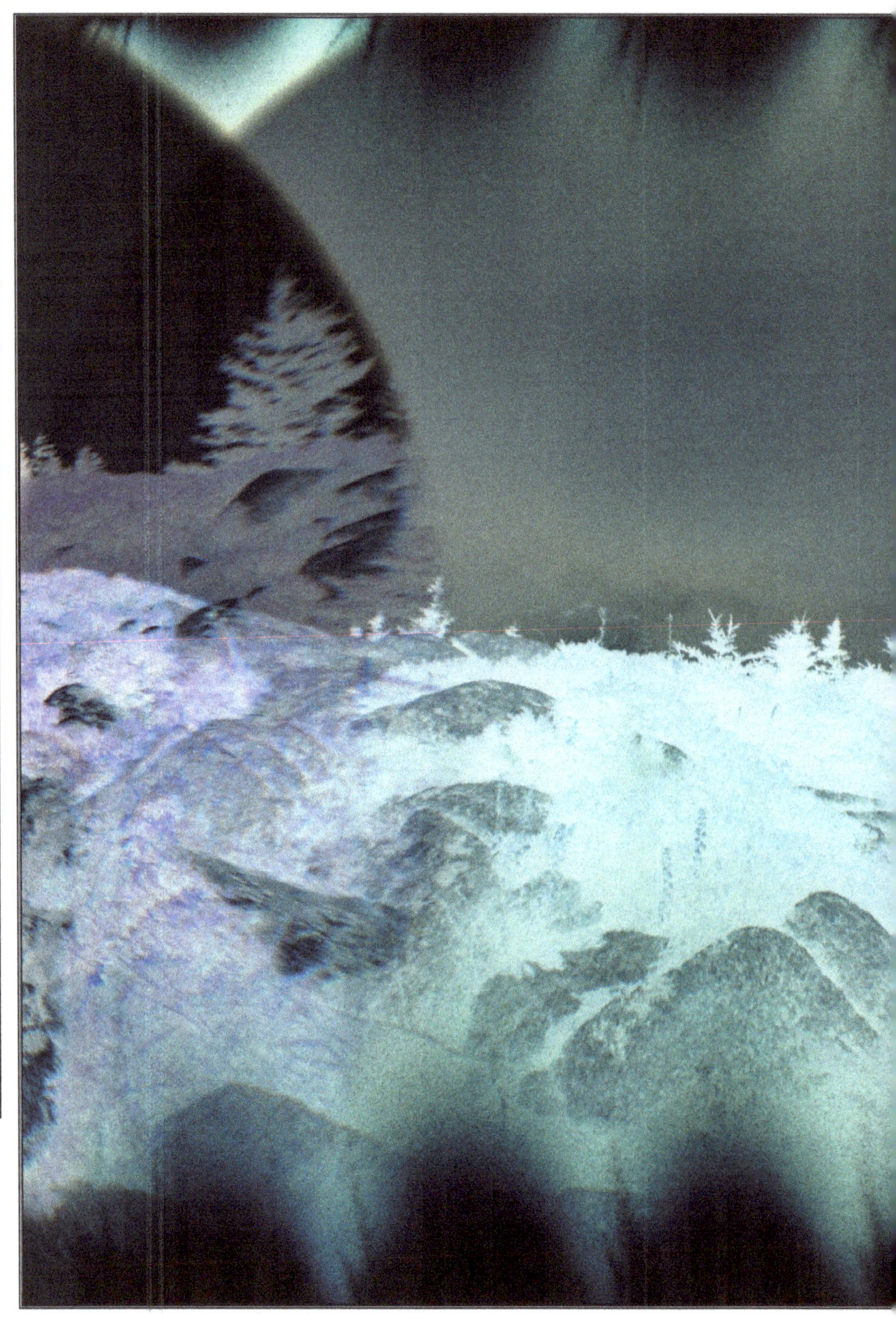

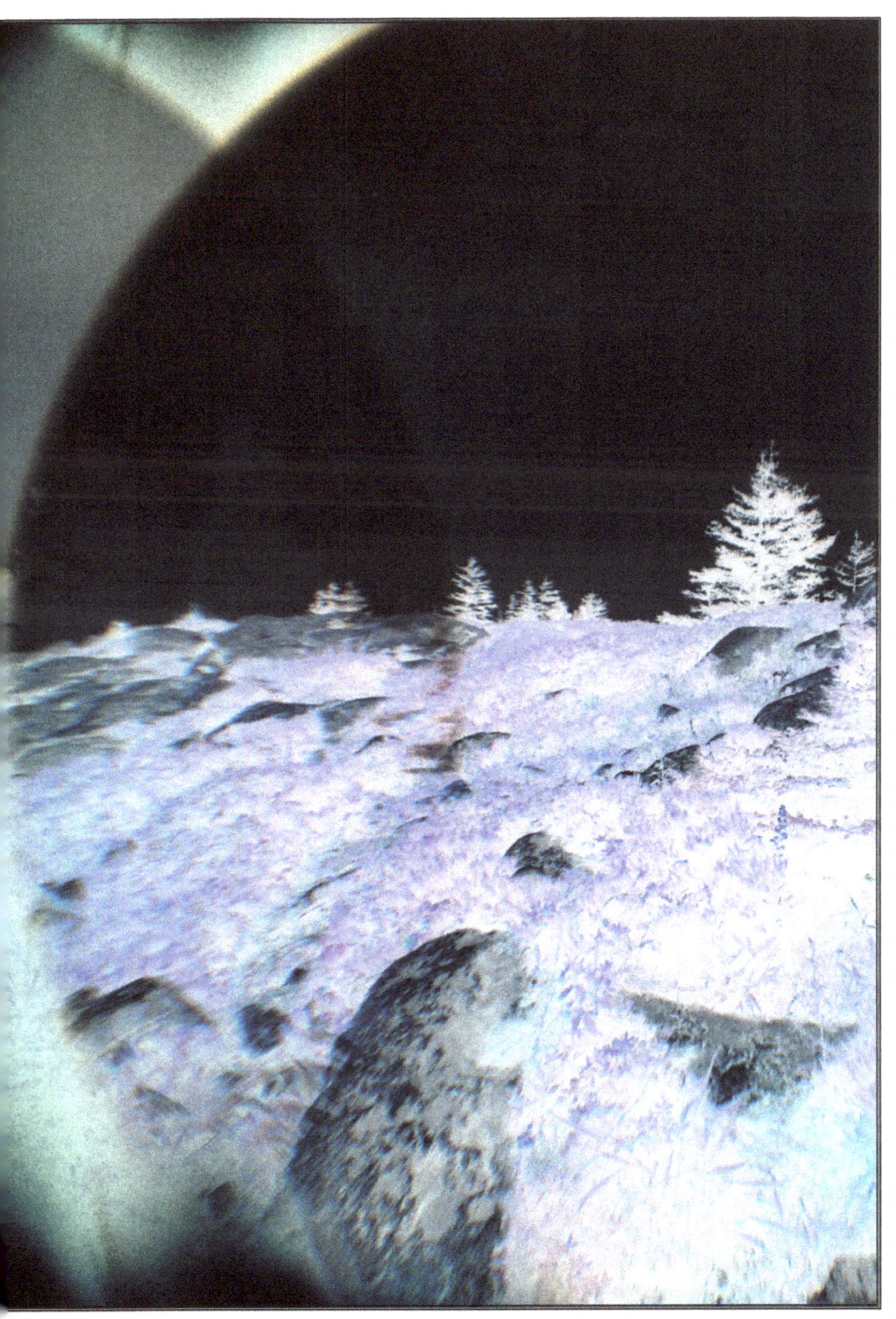

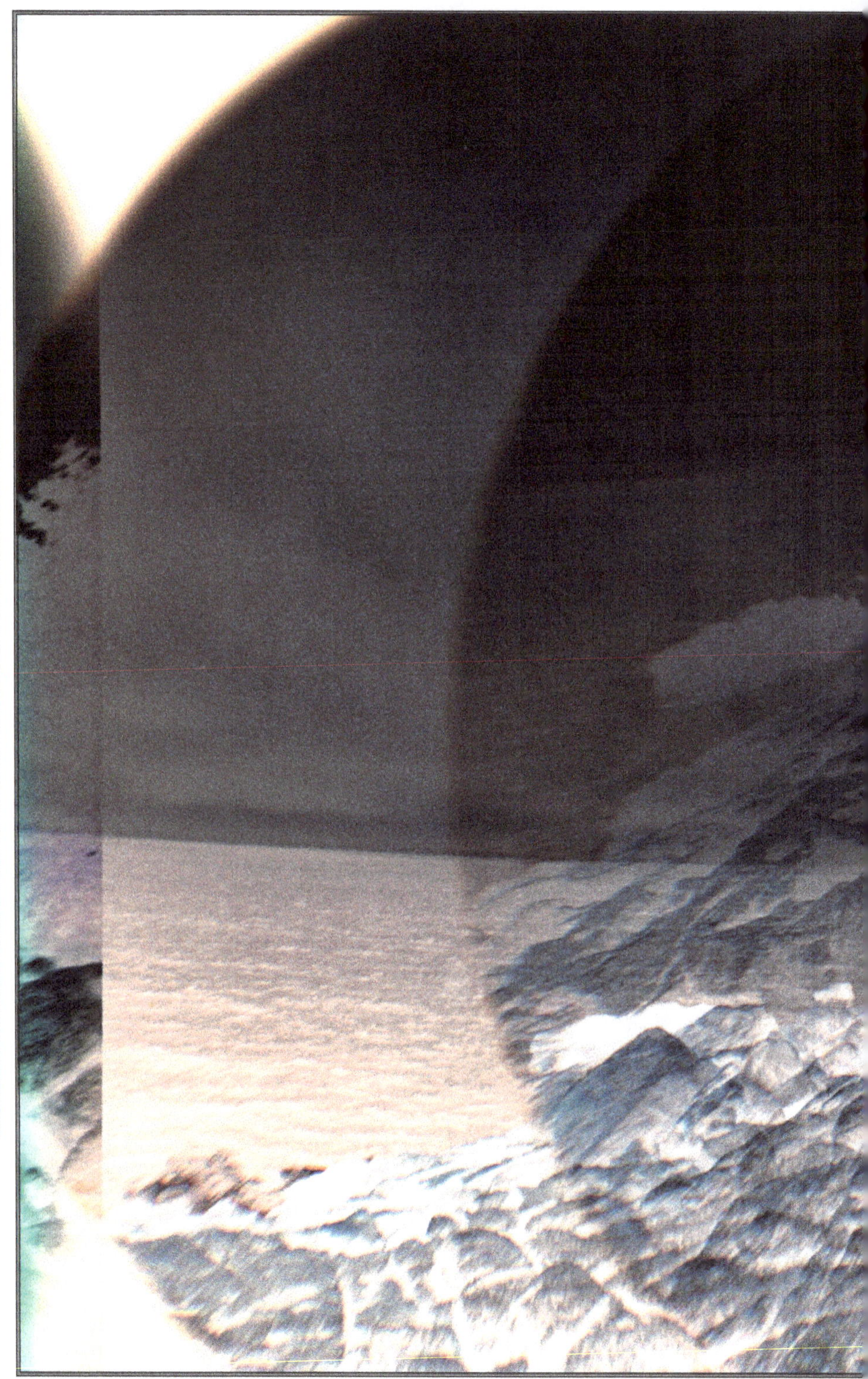

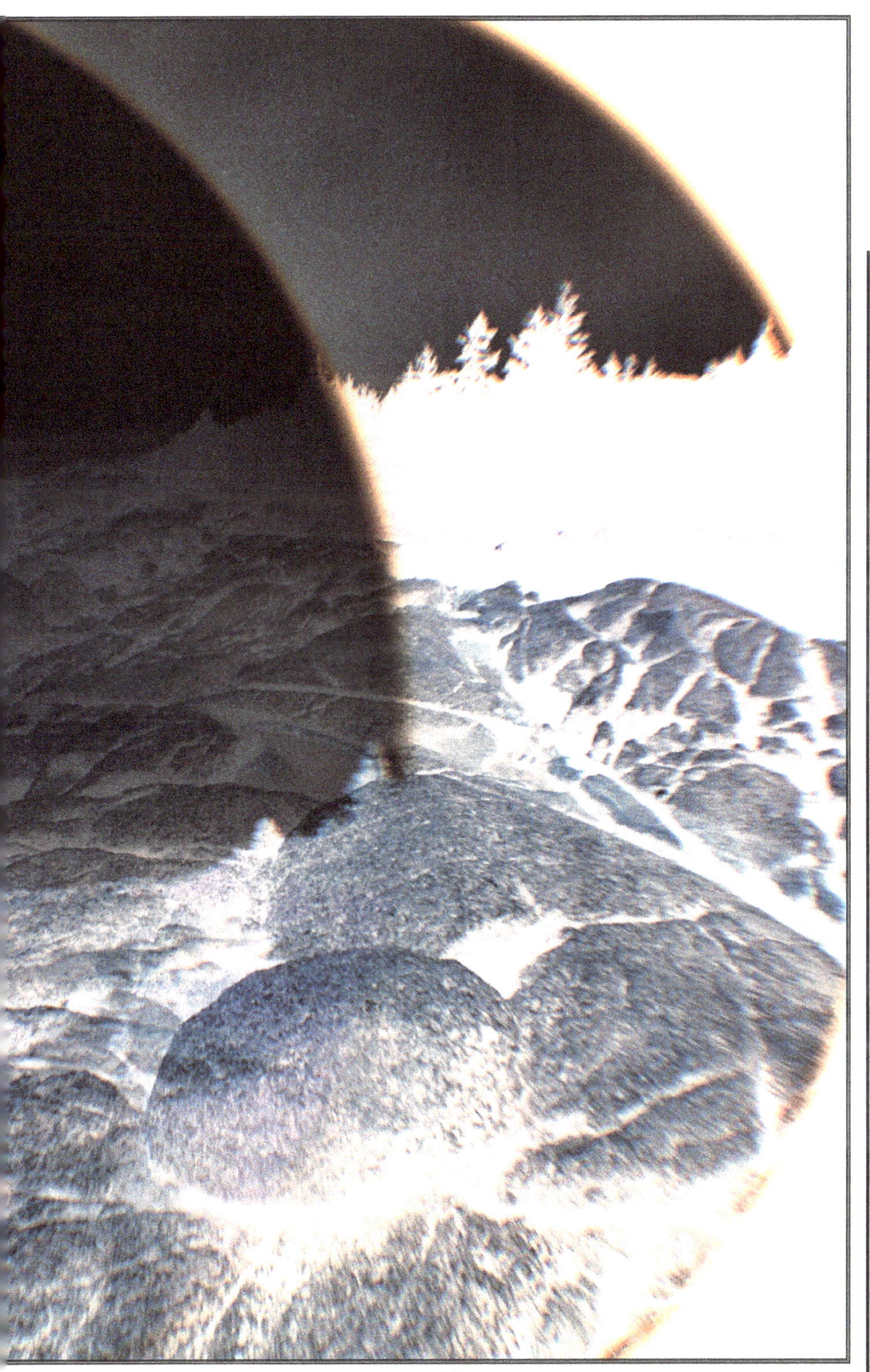

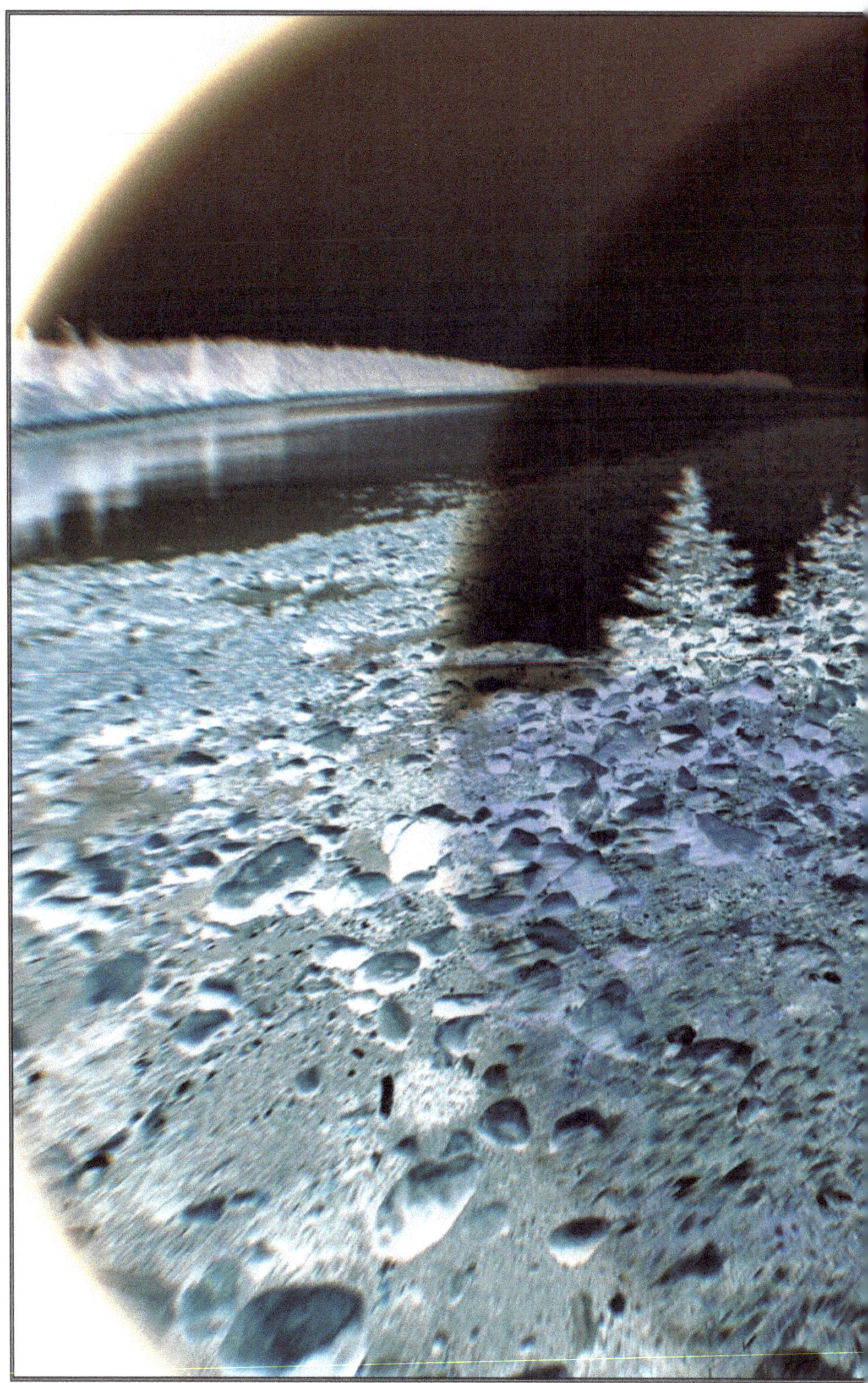

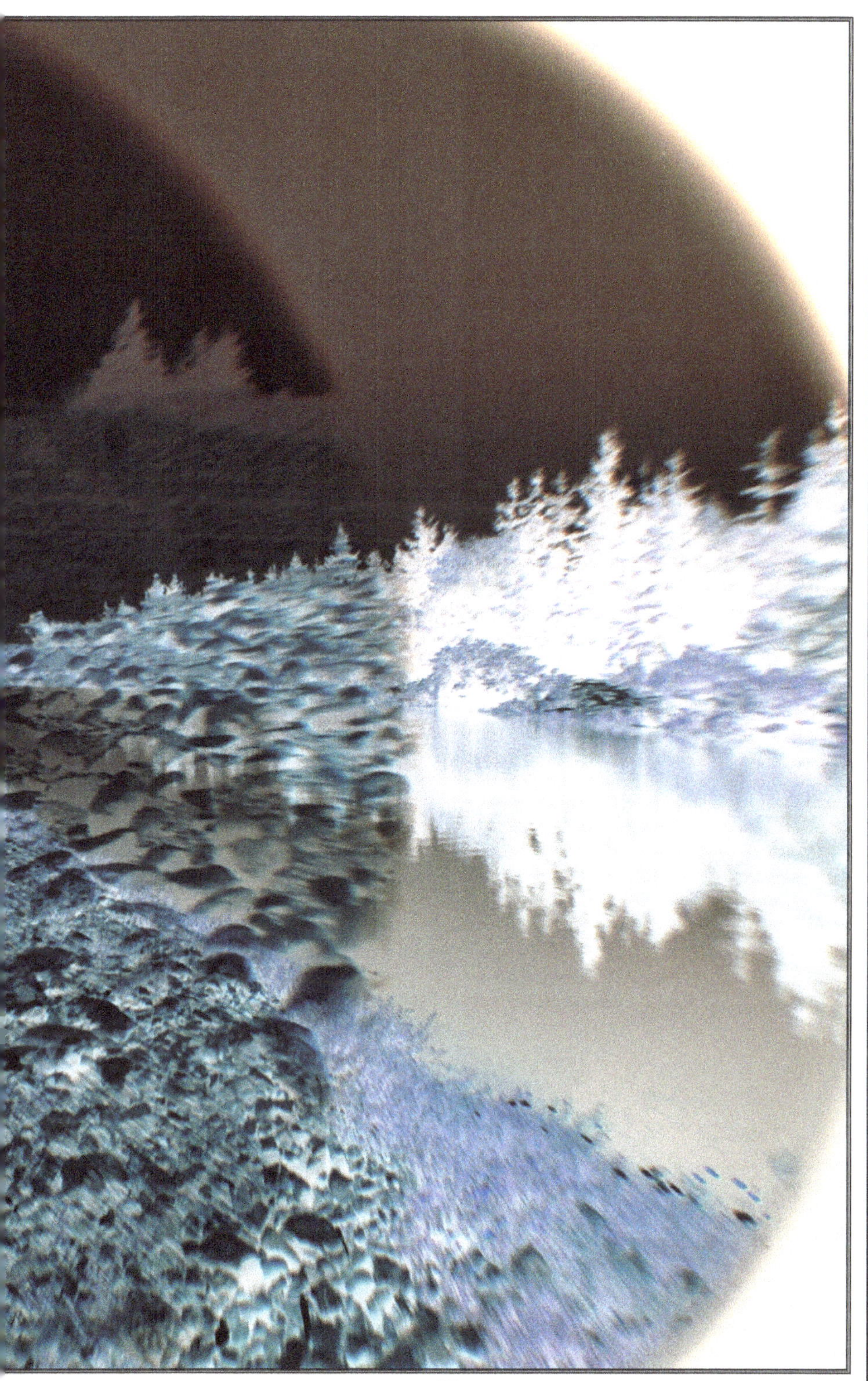

Saint Procla

Mary Sarver

without a name you
appear
only once in
man's gospel
in a single sentence
of Matthew
you exist

but brave
in that space
you testify

your husband
robed in white
yet seated in judgment
bent to your words

you said--
have thou nothing to do
with that just man

did the temerity of your
words cut
like a knife
through Pilate's heart

did he wince?
did his lips tighten in
frustration, his eyes
squeeze shut at
your voice,
ears forced to
hear your pain

did your voice
inspire others
to say--
don't look away from me

to say--
what are you doing, sir
you said--

I have suffered many things this day
in a dream because of him

what did you suffer

your heart breaking
ours

did you know
your words
would do nothing
to stop the horror

but you
chose

to witness
to testify
to confront

Old Jewish Cemetery, Prague

Sarah Gane Burton

How many bodies have you consumed,
O stone-scarred earth,
your face a mass of roots and rock,
your bone-fed grass, a flower
to remember the dead?
For year on year they lifted your skin
of soil to bury a little closer to the surface
another unfortunate soul.
The rain, which purified holy bodies,
twice-washed, board-laid, shroud-clothed,
purifies again the mortal flesh
awaiting resurrection.

Moved From Within

Lee Felty

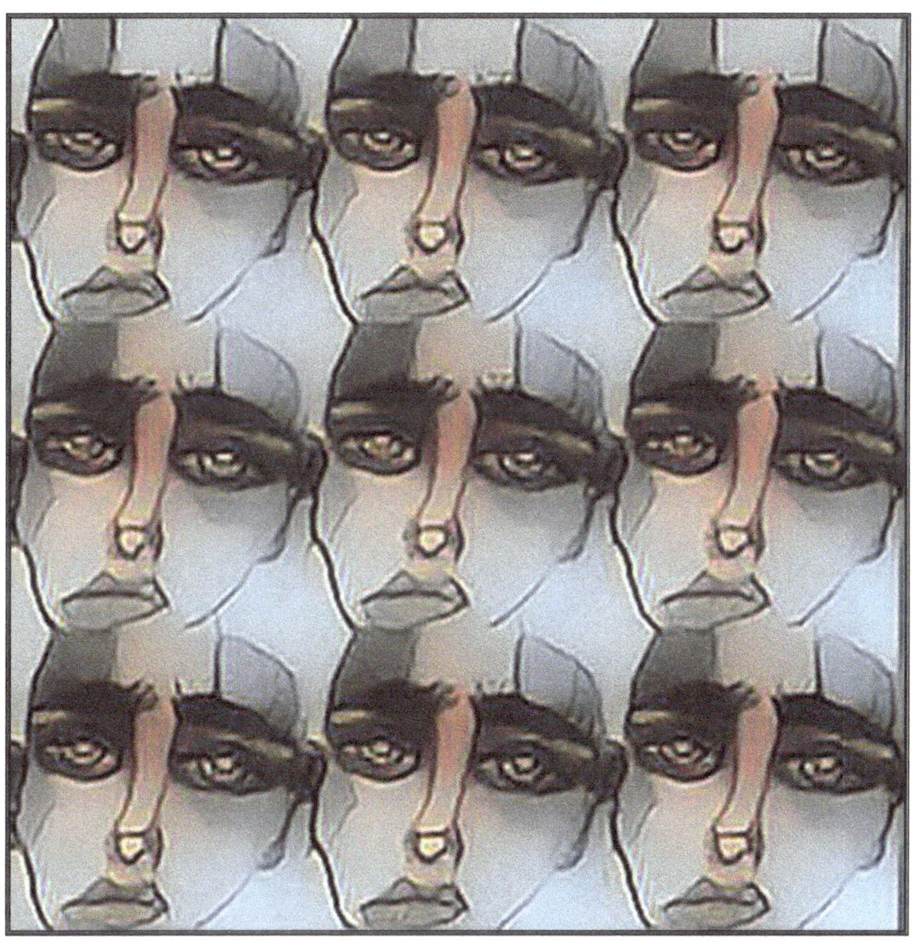

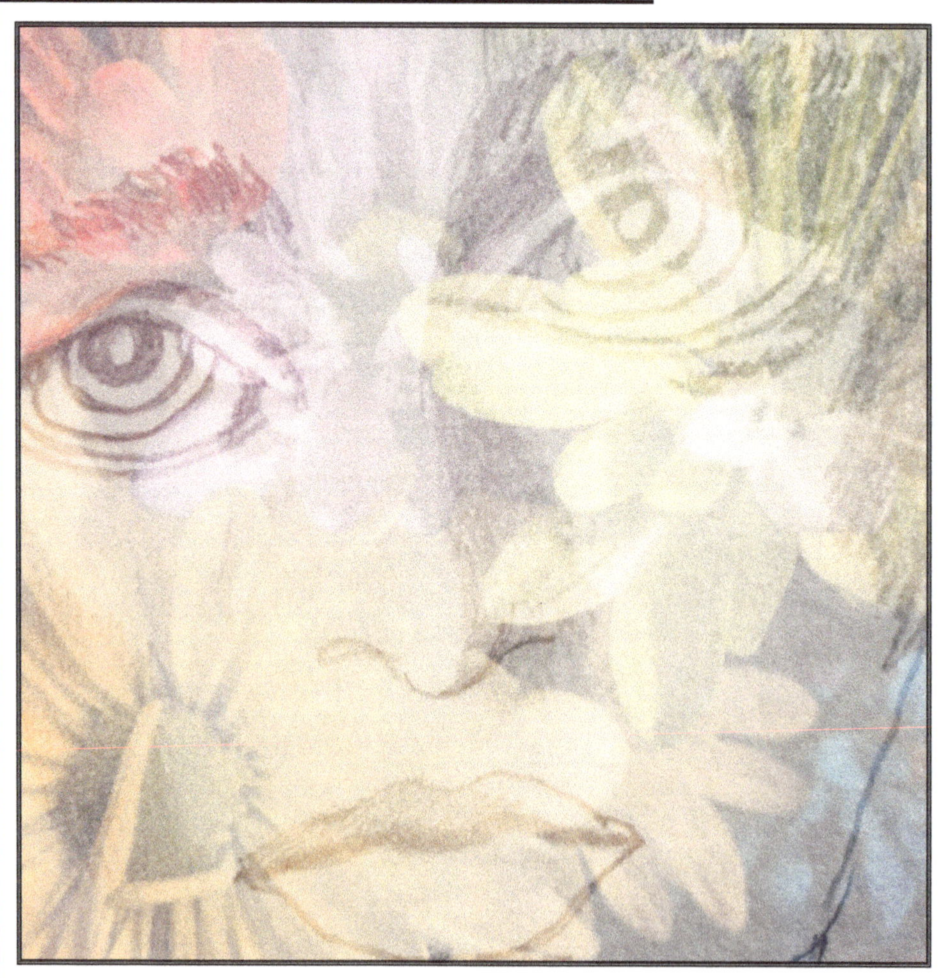

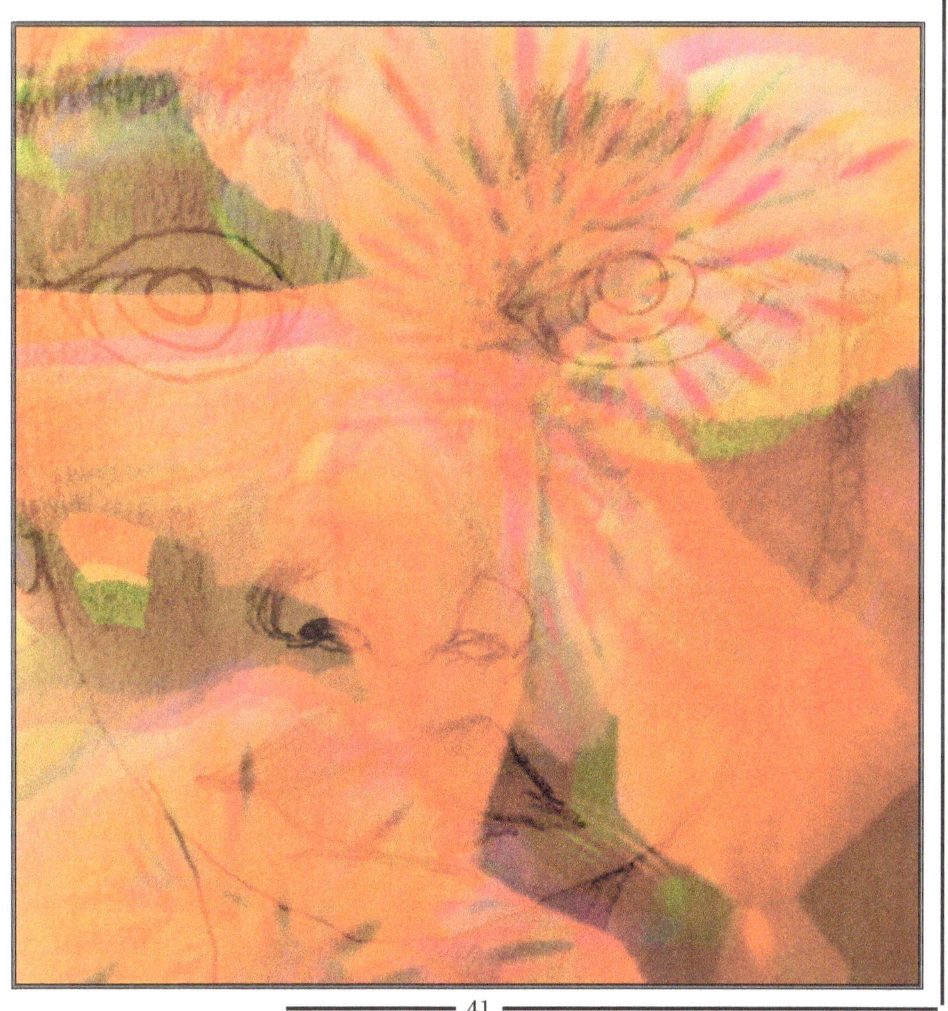

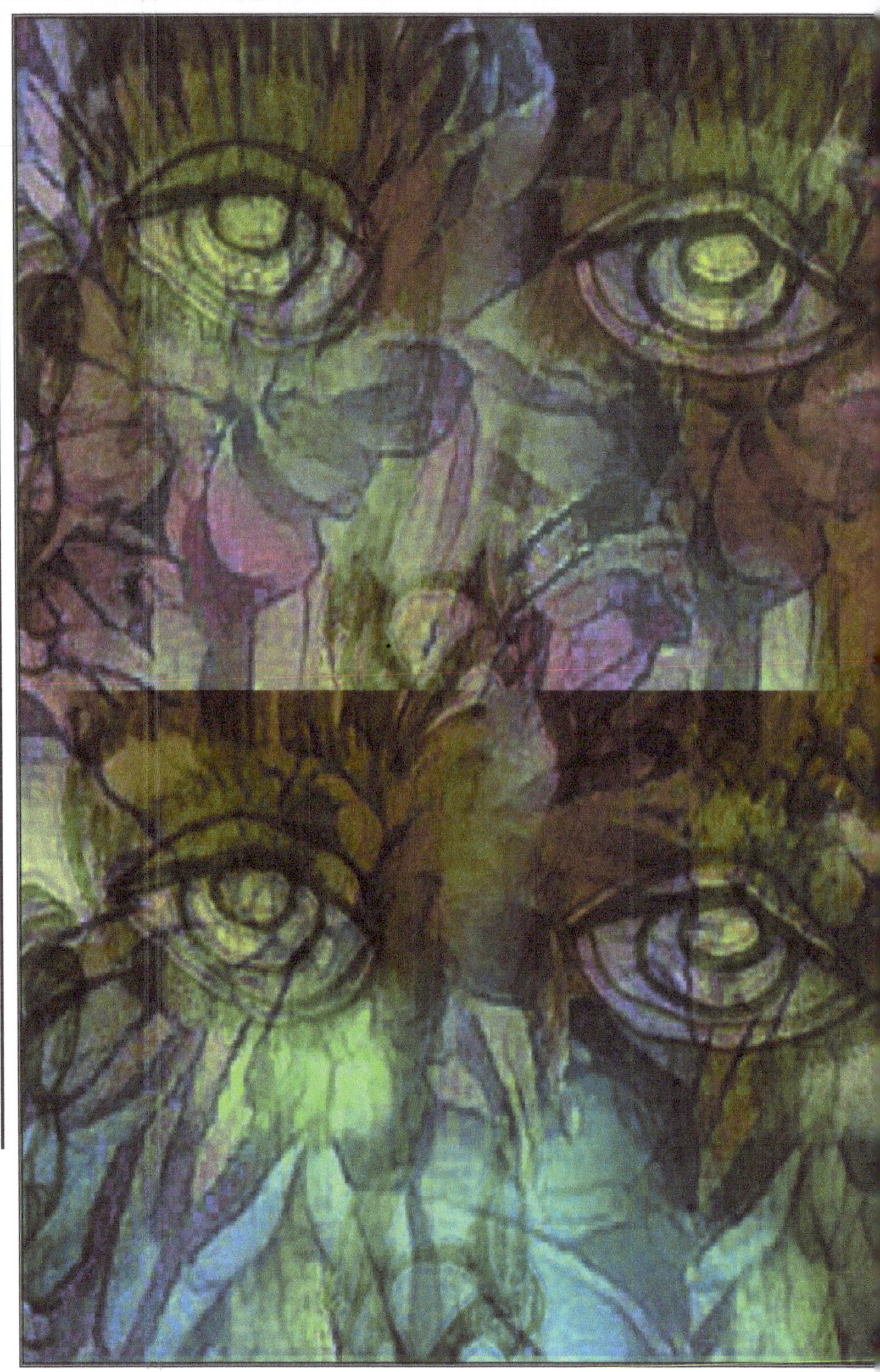

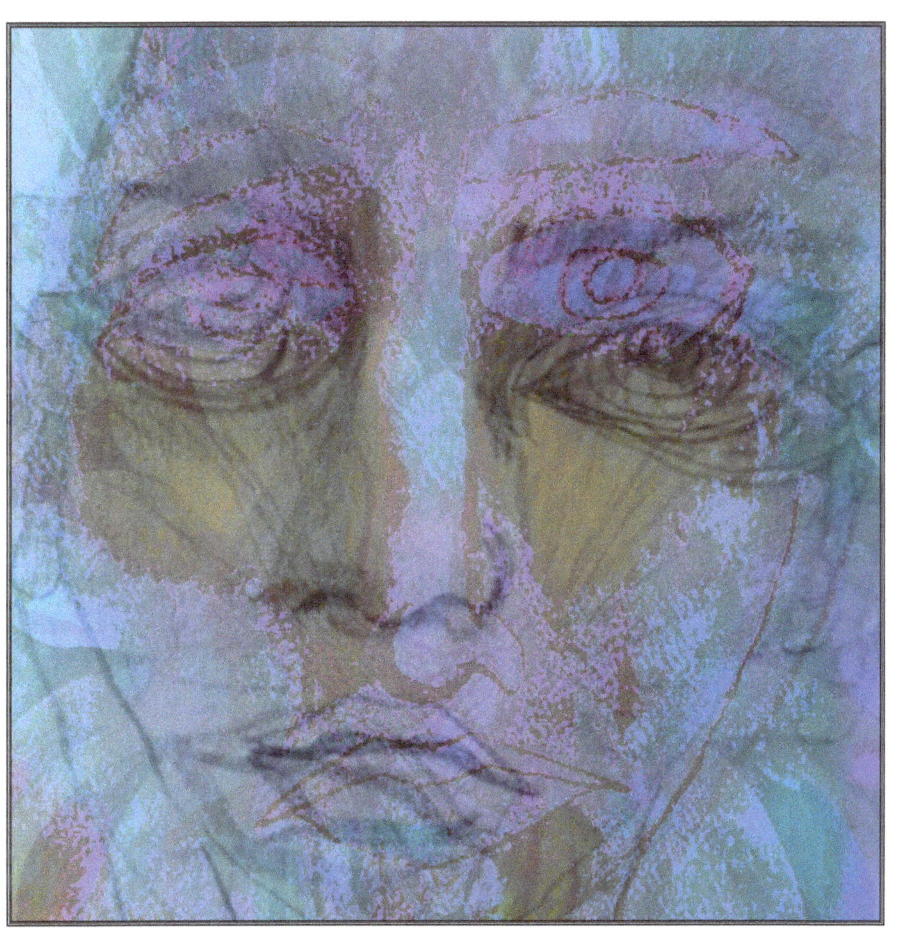

Tomato Sauce

Nadia Farjami

it began with a jar of tomato sauce,
with forgetting her favorite brand;
was it Barilla or Newman's Own?

something plucked
her
memory off
the vines in her brain;
something skinned
her scrapbook,
made it sour

perhaps it was dawn
that dissolved her details,
or maybe even god
that got ahold of her
glands and stuffed
them inside a
genie's bottle

soon, her mind will lose
the sizzle of
hash browns on the stove &
the succulence of
hemingway's words on paper

soon,
the sentences inside
her brain will
become blistered
& acidic

but for now,
it's only
a jar of tomato sauce

Jess says *you look cute in your underwear*
Claire Nelson

flips a silver dollar. The boys undress by the pool.

She is Susan B. Anthony & I'm Apollo Landing
I pee in the bushes.

J says *you win, MoonPie; your call, snack cake*
& I say *Left*; she says *yours or mine?*

I say *mine* only I mean mine
She blinks at Her Right

I get naked for My Left & J's ankle
is gone in the black water & then her calf

reflects light, is gone, her thigh, & she is gone.
My Left is any hands I like. We go under

Left becomes Jess
nibbles my ear, pets me,

I roll my face into her hand.
One black hair is coiled tight on J's breast,

I imagine her lips are mine
only they're mine; tongue coarse hair

tongue mine. J says
let's breakfast, pancakes; get outta here

And I say *nice to meet you* and we are gone.

Shell Game

Holly Woodward

This afternoon, mists shroud the mountains that raised them.

I missed the eclipse, stunned by the obit

of a man I did not know lived.

Each day takes its slice of memory's face.

The moon looks down on us, a clock no hands touch.

What would it cost for a fistful of dust

to sift through our fingertips?

The hands of night must stay gloved.

Clouds film it like the transparent skin

the frog raises over its golden eye

to protect the black pool below.

The eye is a kind of skin—

all senses are touch, even that tiniest bone

in our ears, dangling like a hanged man in the wind.

I remember everything that happened to my lost face.

The stars are not falling to us—we're falling

through them, shards of disasters from our passage.

Under cover of darkness, a curtain of light

flutters in the wake of the sun, as if

night slipped knives from this world to the next.

We give each conflagration a name, or at least

a number, but they should remain unspoken

to mark the loneliness of gods.

Stars need vast emptiness to exist—

you can't get close enough to hear their roar.

Known and strange things pass, catch the heart off guard, and blow it open

Ja Min Yie

Dreams

Victoria Parker

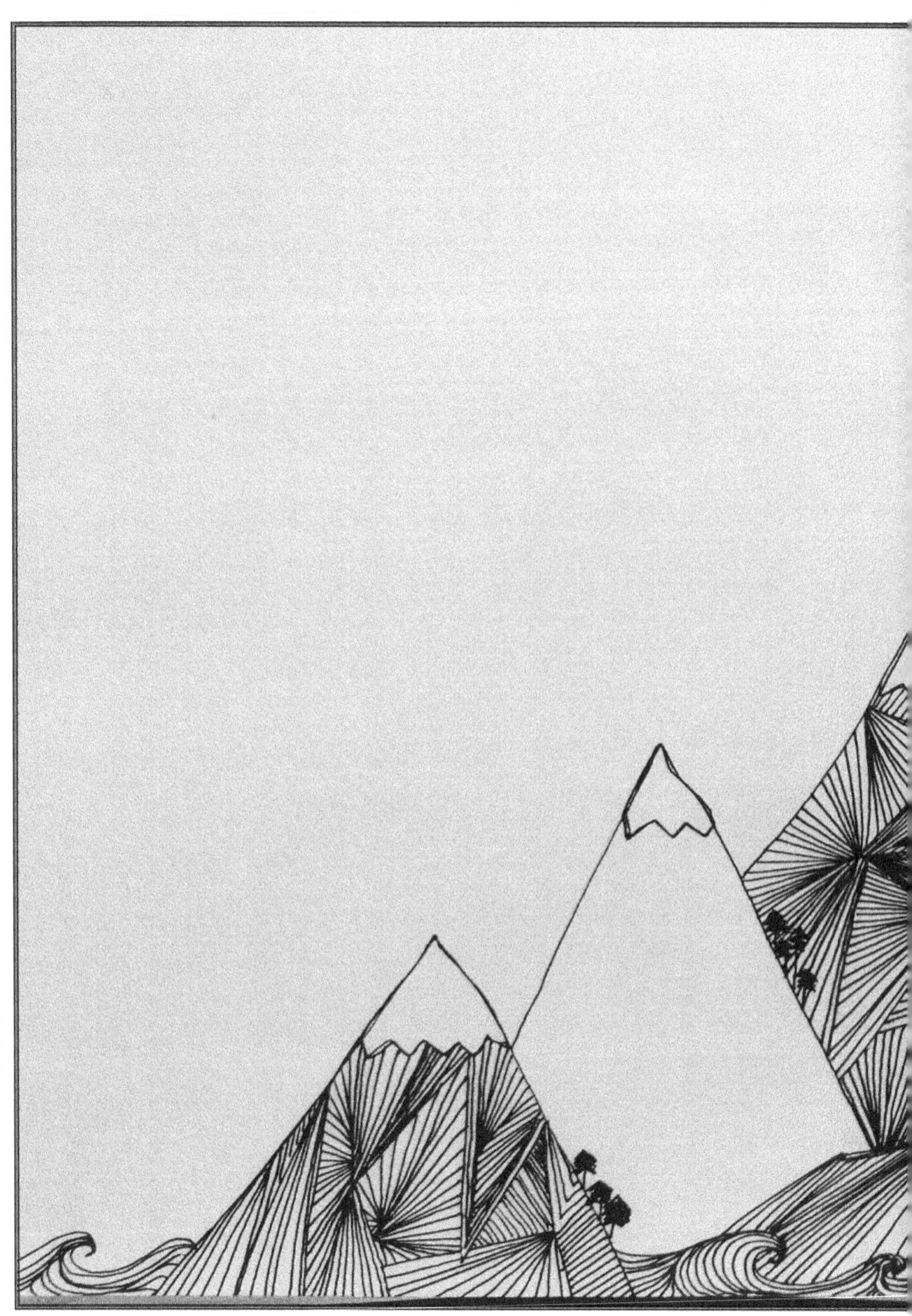

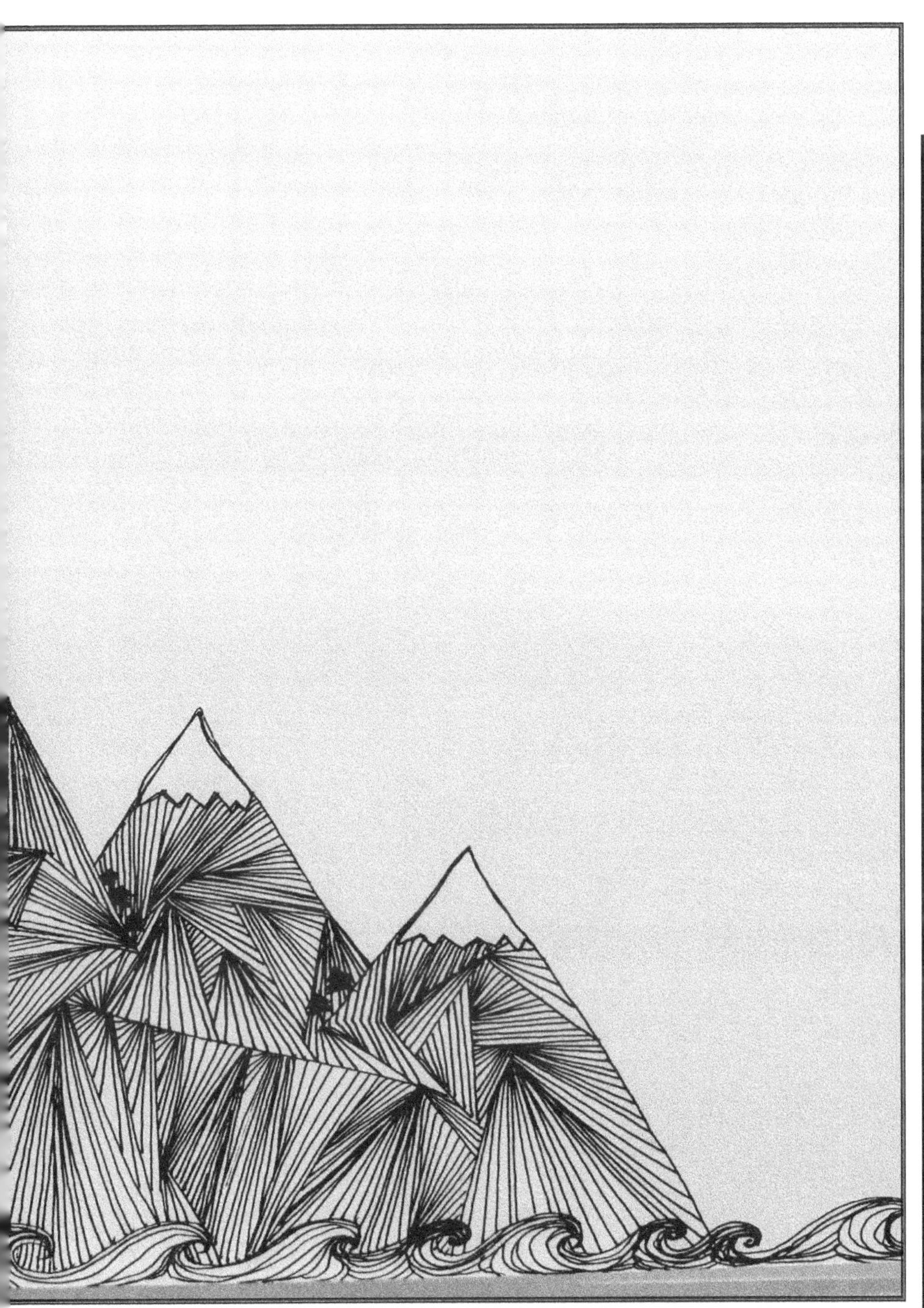

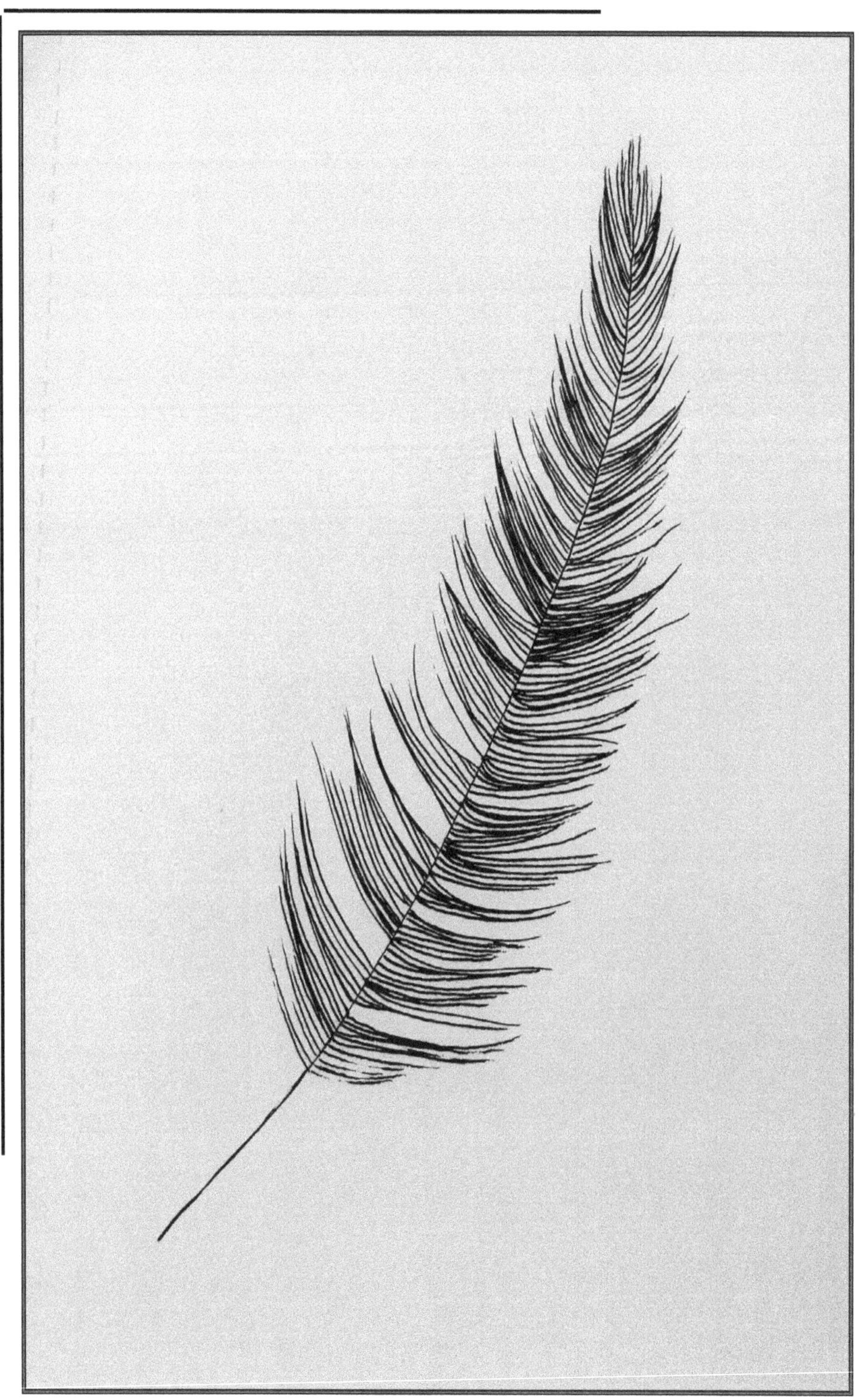

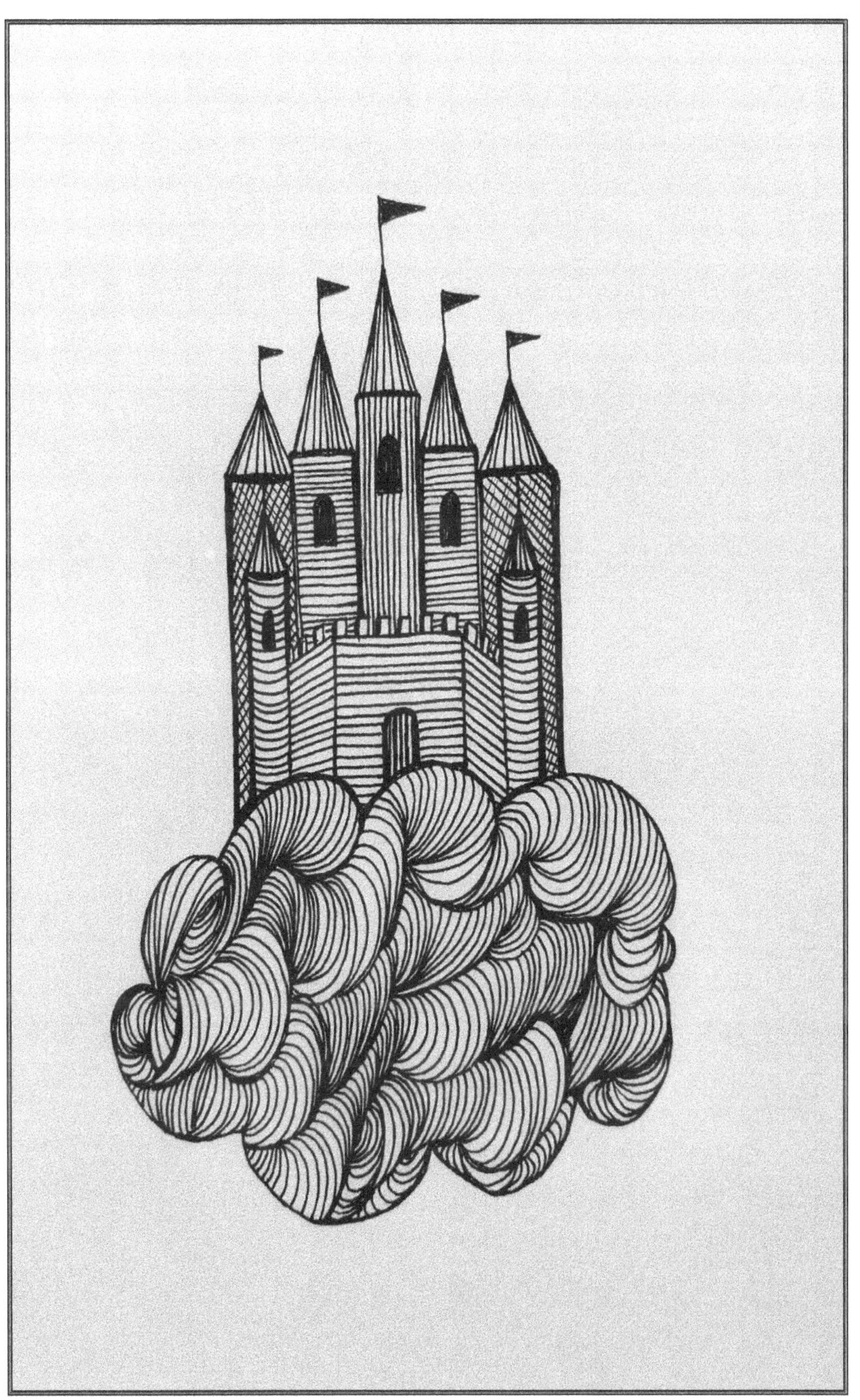

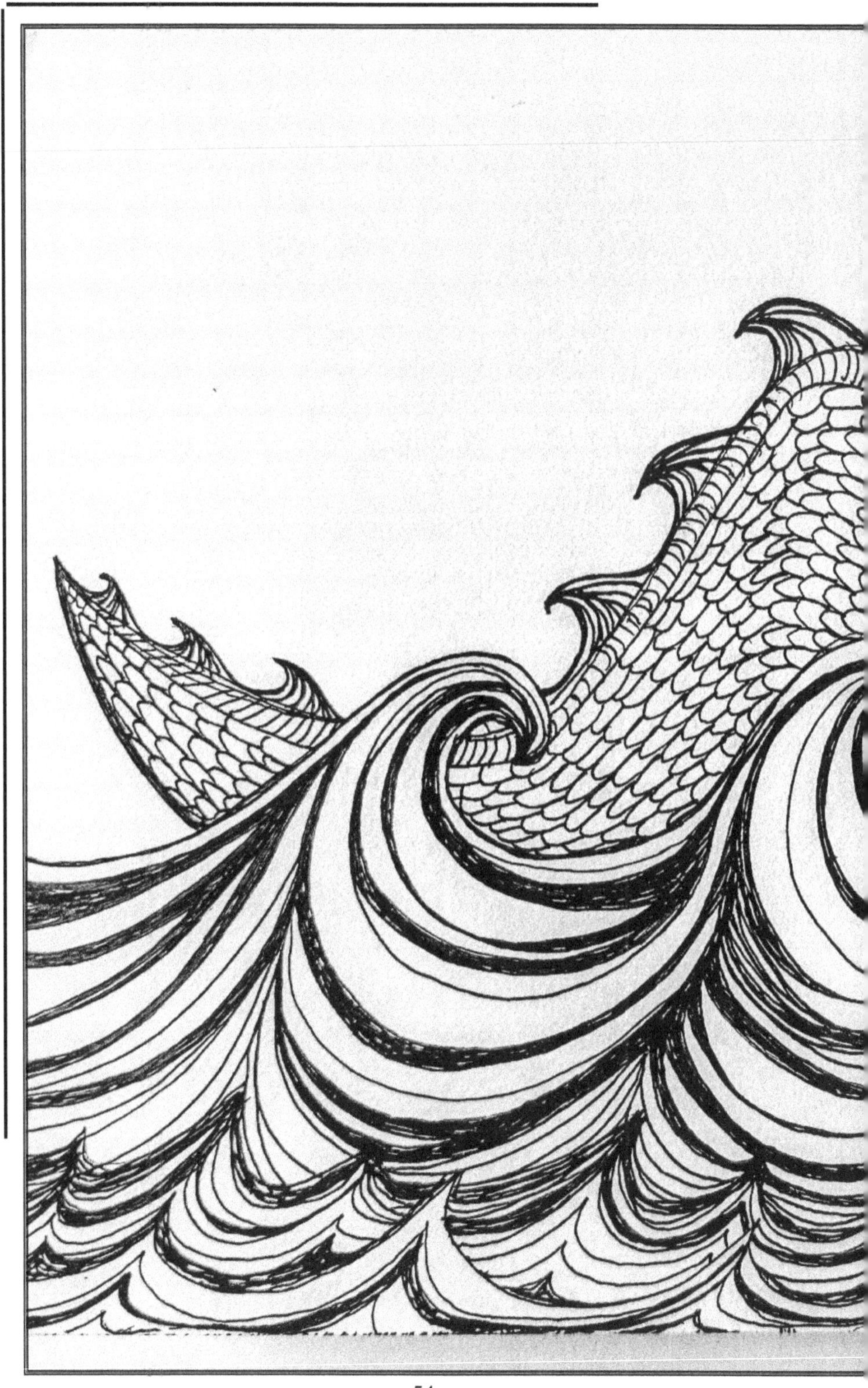

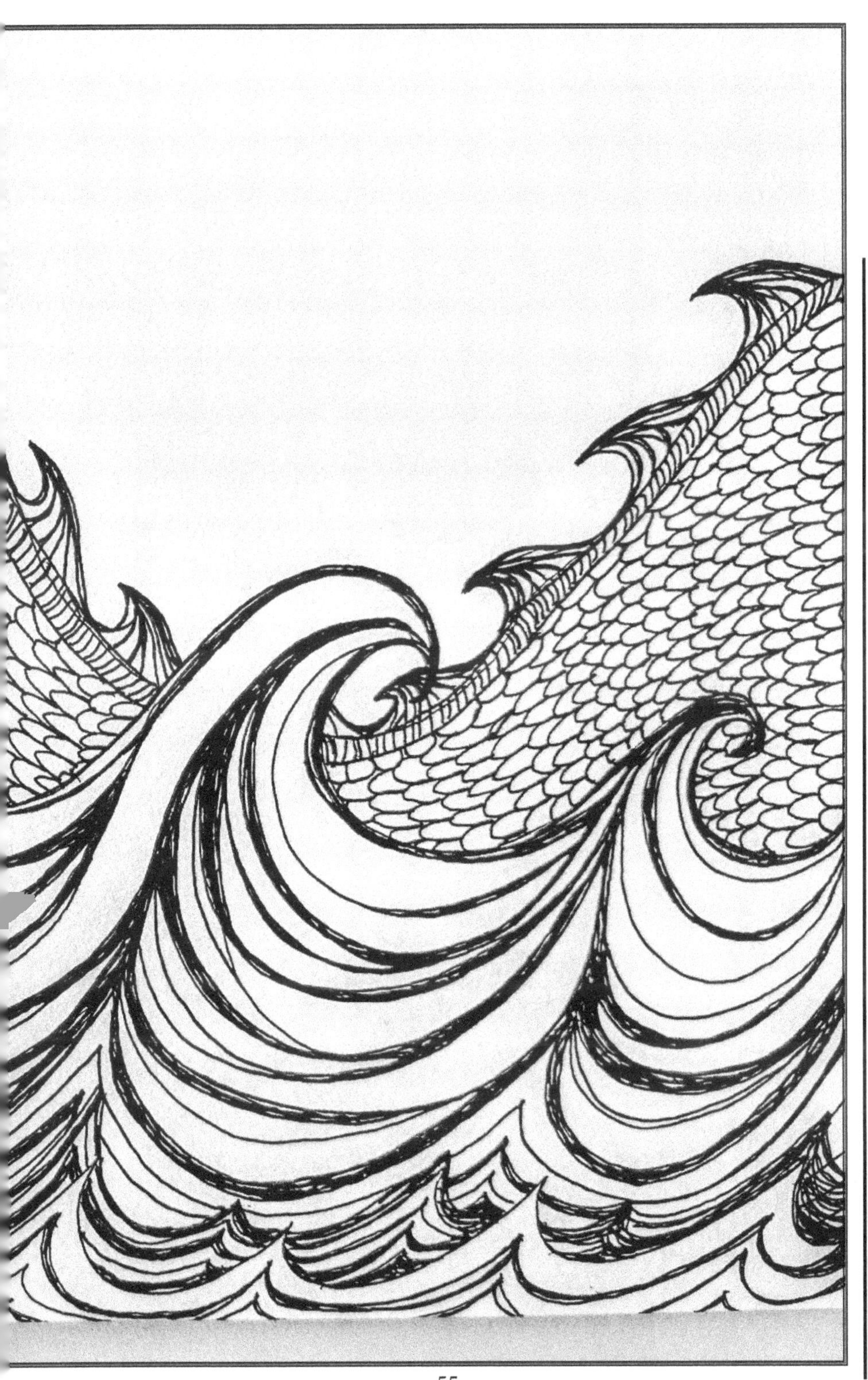

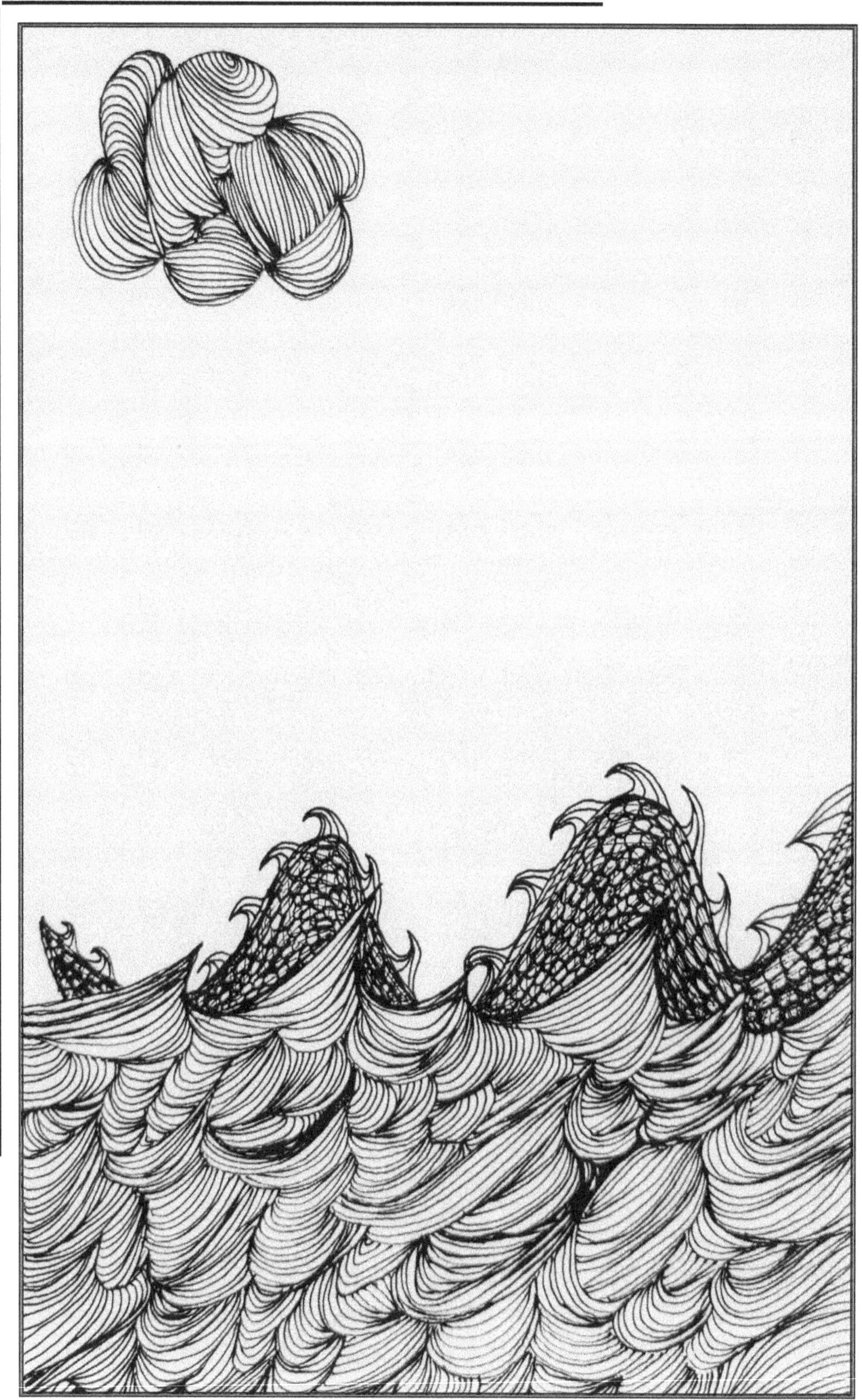

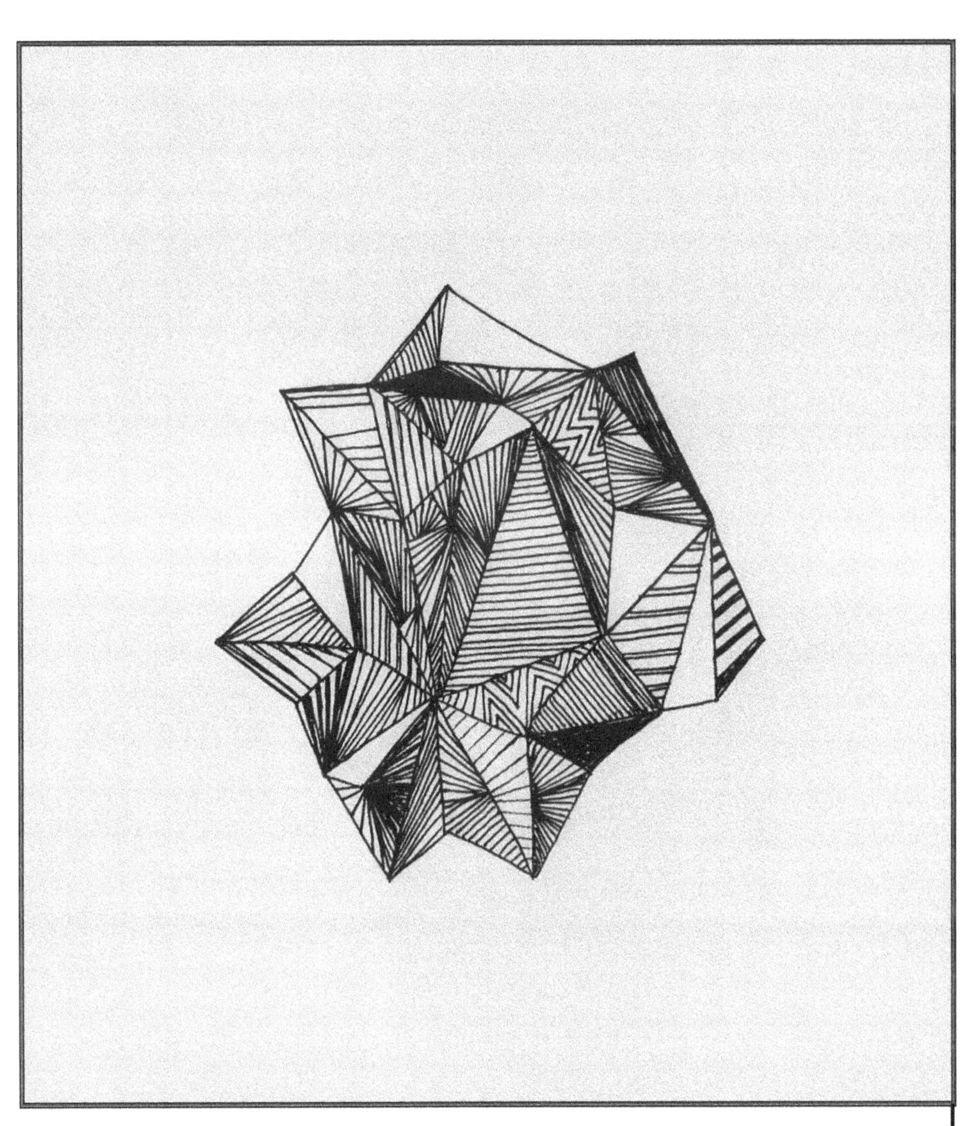

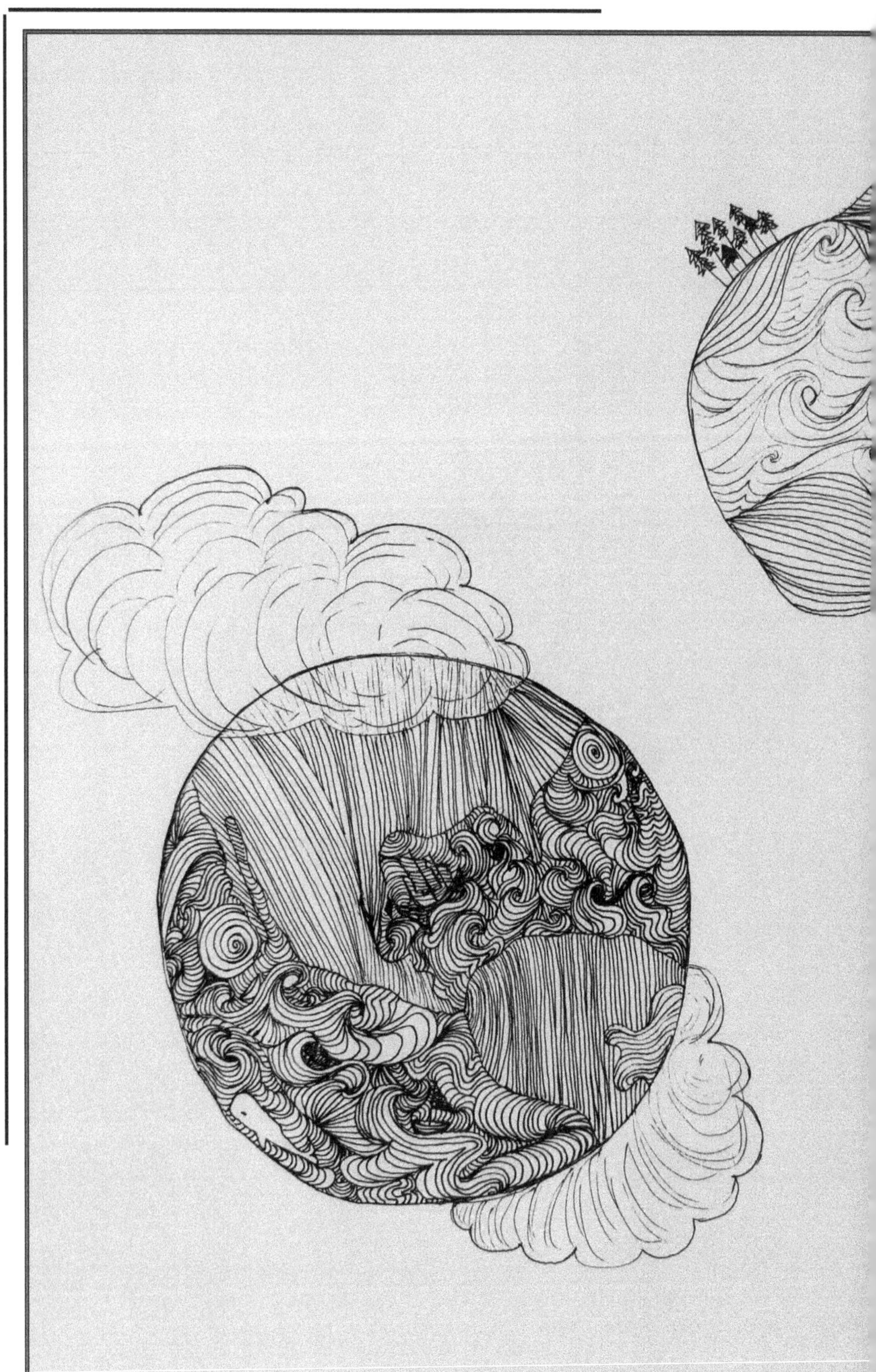

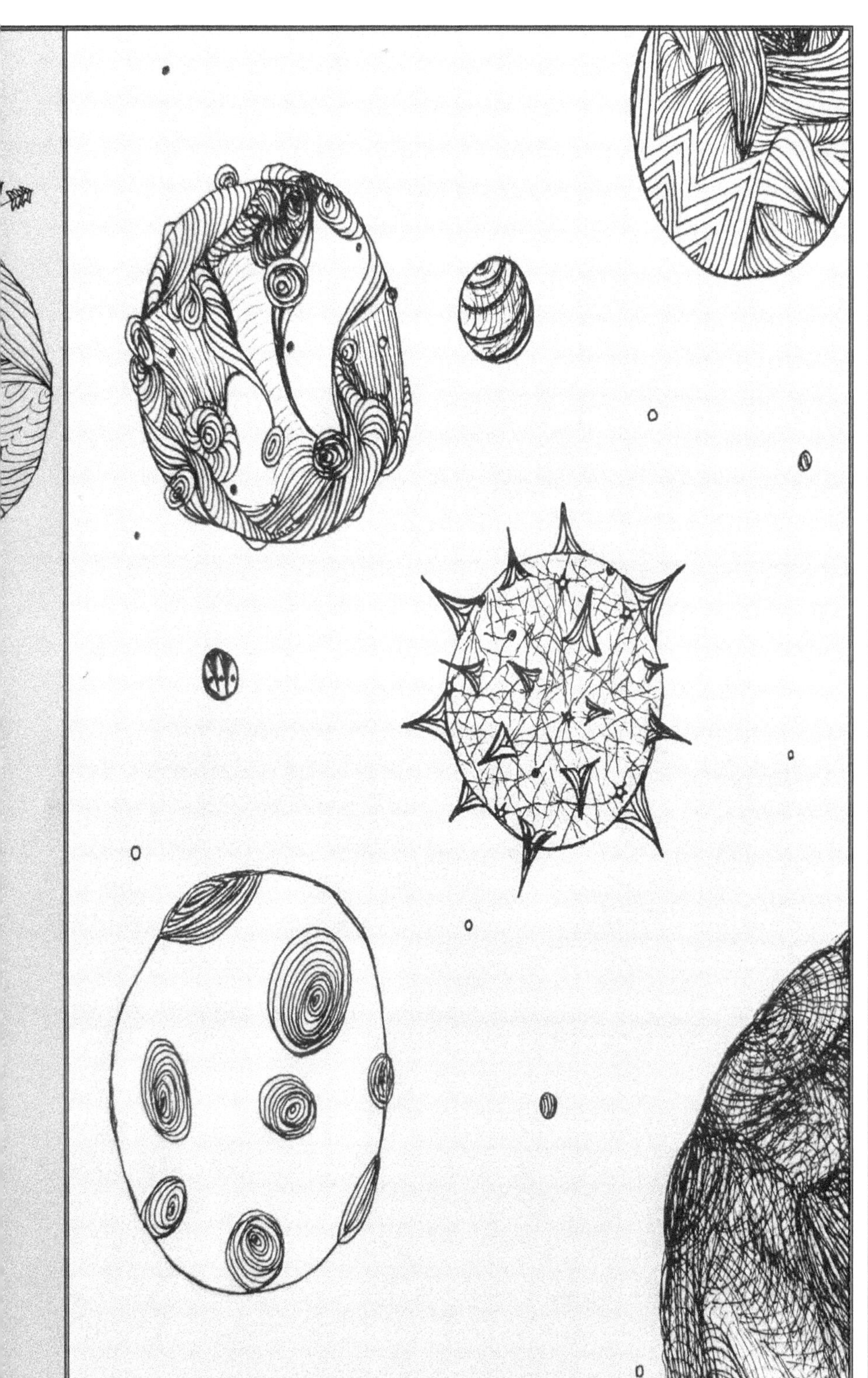

Harami Nala

Basmah Sakrani

Shock-and-awe headlines of abandoned boats: empty vehicles
of action, all bark and masculine like the unwanted gaze of
your teacher, an older cousin, the tailor who stitched together a
periwinkle lehenga for you to twirl in, even as he pinned you,
days before your brother's wedding, against a leaning iron-
board heaving with other women's half-formed dresses.

A numbers game: won by the British long ago, but played
today by two halves of a whole who postulate as if contributing
to high art.

A he said-he said war: of vanished fishermen leaving behind
trawlers that their wives will crawl for a scent or a forgotten
washcloth.

Will they rejoice, any of them?

Quicksand: shins caked in the sloppy debris of secrets of the
state that turn into missives and missiles before you'll have a
chance to visit the salt flats where travelers lose their ways,
drawn by the dancing lights of chir batti like a woman
possessed with revenge and a hunger to lure and leech.

No man's land: a hyphen in the Arabian Sea where once,
centuries ago, your forefathers staked an ounce of blood into
the land – a claim without cartography – that spills now from
your pen, sprouting with no warning to make you pause where
it hurts even as you cry out the question burning holes in your
tongue.

But what of the foremothers?

to be

Jon Cribb

is owns its presence.
is is and can be was
is is absolute certainty.
to be is itself a powerful.
state   of   being.

is was and is important to literature.
is defines and illustrates character.
is is not a comparison as as is
is can no longer be just a
"helping   verb"

"is or not is
that to be the question"

The Tyranny of Quirks

Chris Andrews

In the lost masterwork of Melbourne fumblecore
set in the summer when the shuffle met the bounce,
there are hesitations so patiently rehearsed
you'd swear the actors were winging it or blanking.
The whole stunt / accident distinction collapses
in an unspectacular way on the dancefloor,
any surface, that is, with the requisite slip.
Microphones got buried in leisurewear, so when
from the depths of hood and couch our lost heroine
sums up the lesson of the seminar, it sounds
like stuttering: 'Posers of posers are posers.'
One review was titled, 'The Tyranny of Quirks.'
The one. I'm not saying it was hard to be snide
about those nicely put-together young people
savouring the privilege of disillusion
in a world where most don't even get what it was
they thought they wanted. But I have not forgotten
a scene singled out for its sheer self-indulgence:
Who is this not even secondary character
puttering wearily amid party jetsam,
purging ash and dregs, momentarily tempted
by thimblefuls of distillate but saved by yawns,
while a far magpie descants, and the light balance
tips imperceptibly from lamp to paling sky?
And another scene, dismissed as 'decoration':
a man comes up the street in a wheelchair shouting:
'I want to walk again. I want to *fucking walk!*'
and some nimble hand–held camera operating
shows how two tenants of the standard miracle
are broken in their strides and don't know where to look.

Chronic Hypochondriac

James Ph. Kotsybar

She finally saw the specialist who
told her to stop diagnosing herself.

She'd no macular degeneration --
just eyestrain from searching the internet,
and her kidneys were not about to fail;
She only needed proper hydration.

Though she got prescriptions to aid her ills,
she hasn't made it to the pharmacy.

The important thing is she's not dying.
She'll get the medications tomorrow,
unless her agoraphobia wins,
and depression keeps her in bed all day.

Inactivity's bedsores, however
will need researching, lest they be cancer.

On My Way To The Doctor

Stephen Nathan

disheveled
on my way to glimpse my uncertain future
I see you walking toward me through the sidewalk swarm
we used to be friends
inseparable
until the ruse of time
stole the years and dissolved us
no one's fault perhaps
and now...
I smile at the sight of you revealed through the crowd
a wish granted I never knew I made
and you see
the surprise of me surfaces for you with a wave and quickened pace
the city's racket cresting washing over us
cleansing everything but this moment
and we hug with years of unspent affection

you look good I say
(he does
robust athletic genetically cheerful)
so do you he lies
Christ how long has it been
Danny's party before I left for Brazil
we talk quickly
trying to sweep up the spilled years
running down the list of questions we all have in reserve
job kids mates apartments
and stop for a breath when we run out of details
all useless really
just providing the sounds we're swapping
like birds
to let each feel the union
the intercourse of the moment
we're usually too guarded to share
I'm so sorry I slept with your wife I don't say
hoping he never looked in that drawer
his eyes are vast and say he doesn't know
it's mine alone
another deed that festers in me
another small bomb of regret
perhaps one reason I have this appointment

we have to get together he says
a dinner
I'd love that I say
and we both mean it
both believe we can reel in the past and make it now
at least I do

another hug
time kindly stopping again

and you're doing well he asks
studying my astigmatic appearance with concern now
yeah yeah just coming from the gym didn't have time to shower I lied
good then good
yeah good you too
I'm the same contact info
me too
so...

once more we wrap ourselves in each other
soon he says
yes soon I hope
and filled with the warmth of us
I walk to the doctor to discuss my options.

Mixed Media Musings

Kelly Schaub

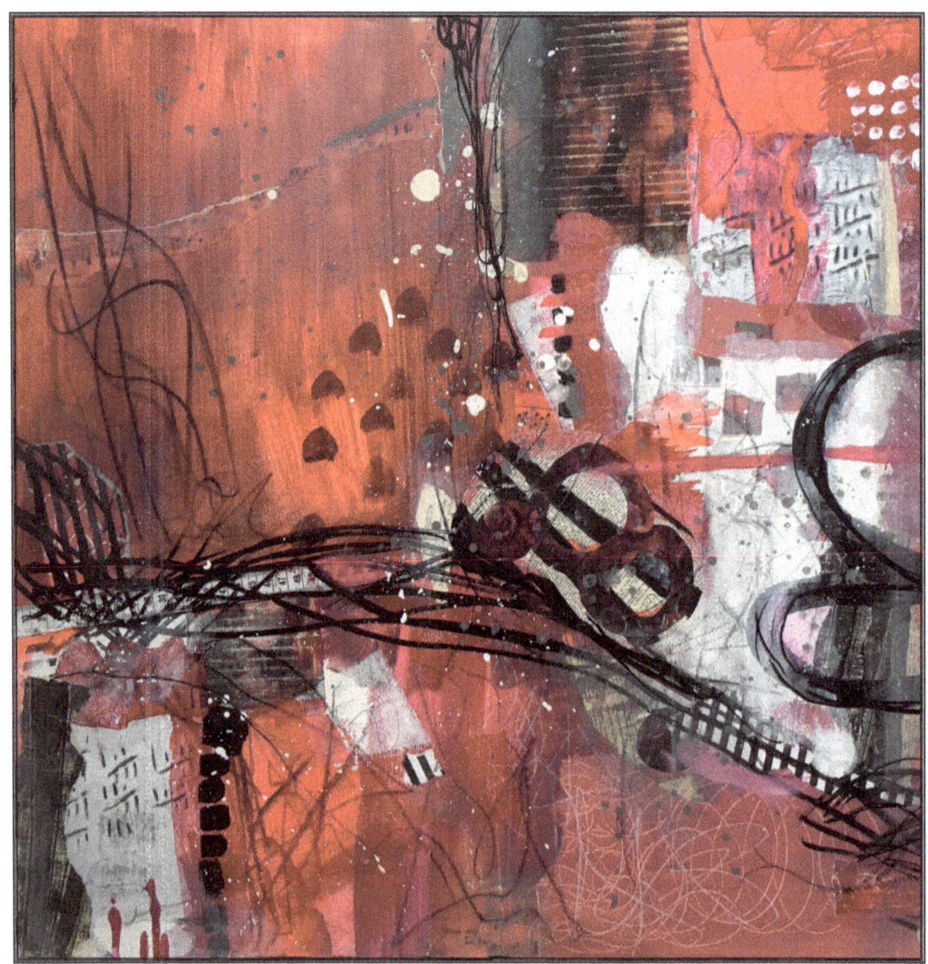

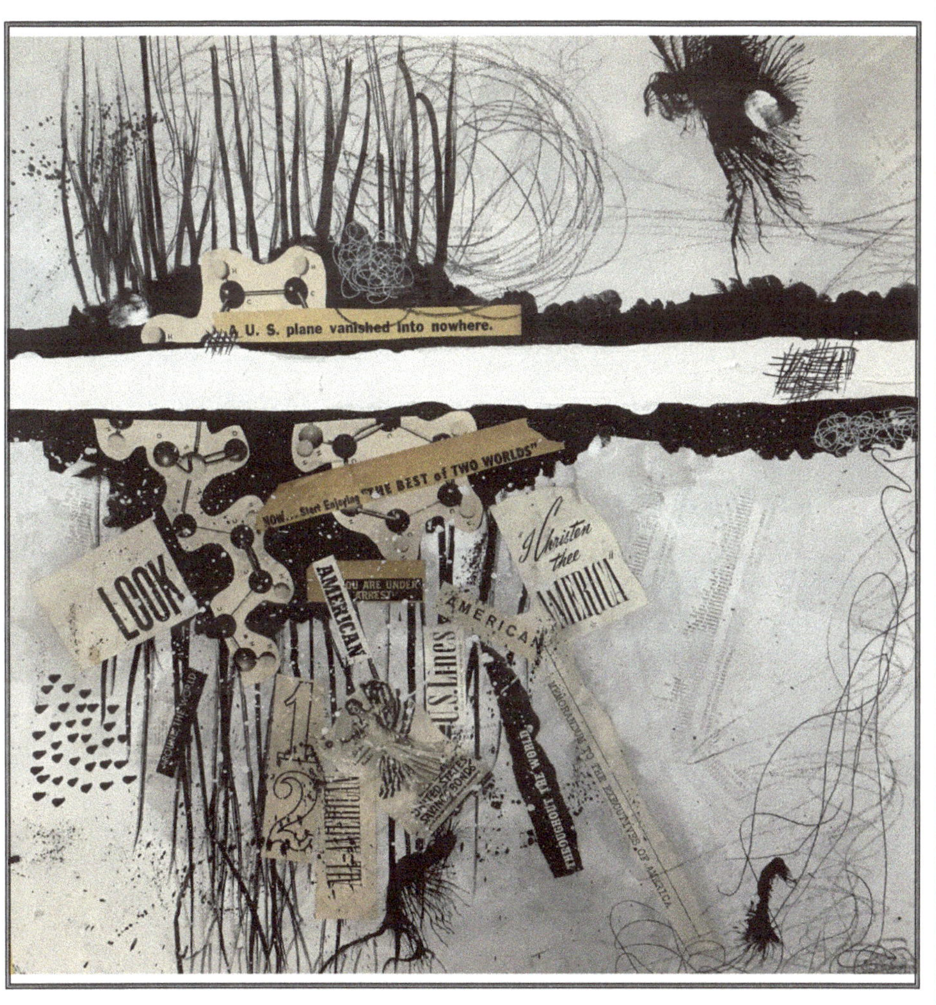

A U. S. plane vanished into nowhere.
NOW....Start Enjoying "THE BEST of TWO WORLDS"
"I Christen thee AMERICA"
LOOK
AMERICAN
YOU ARE UNDER ARREST
AMERICAN
U.S. LINES
UNITED STATES SAVINGS BONDS

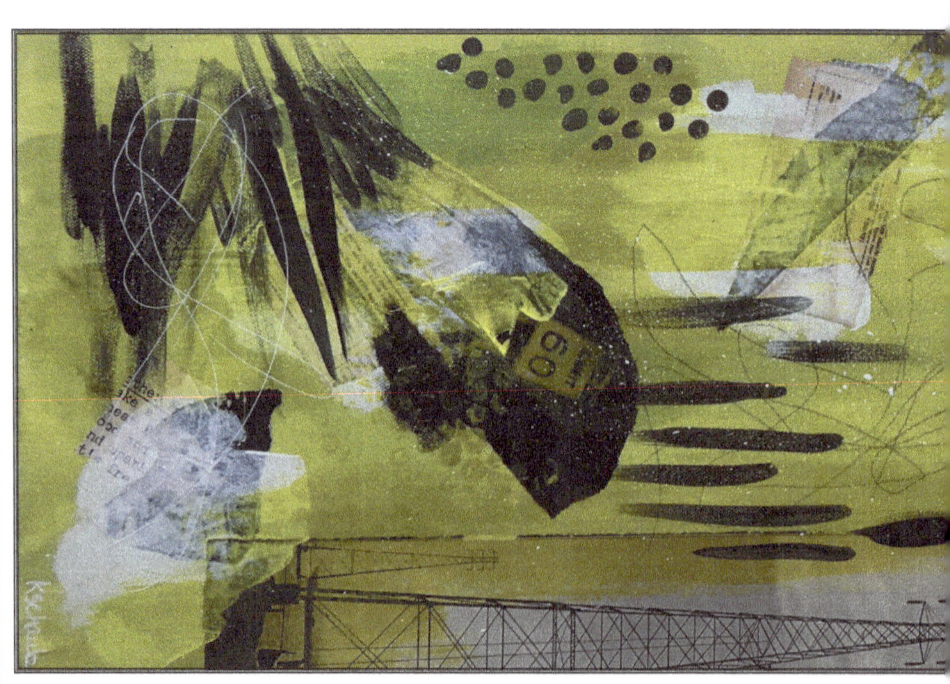

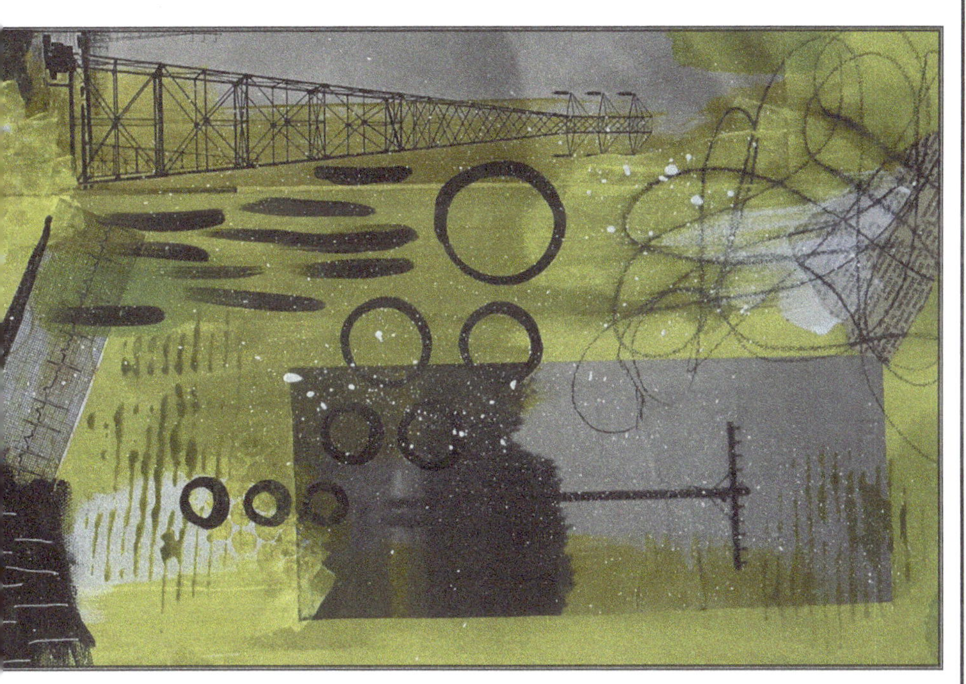

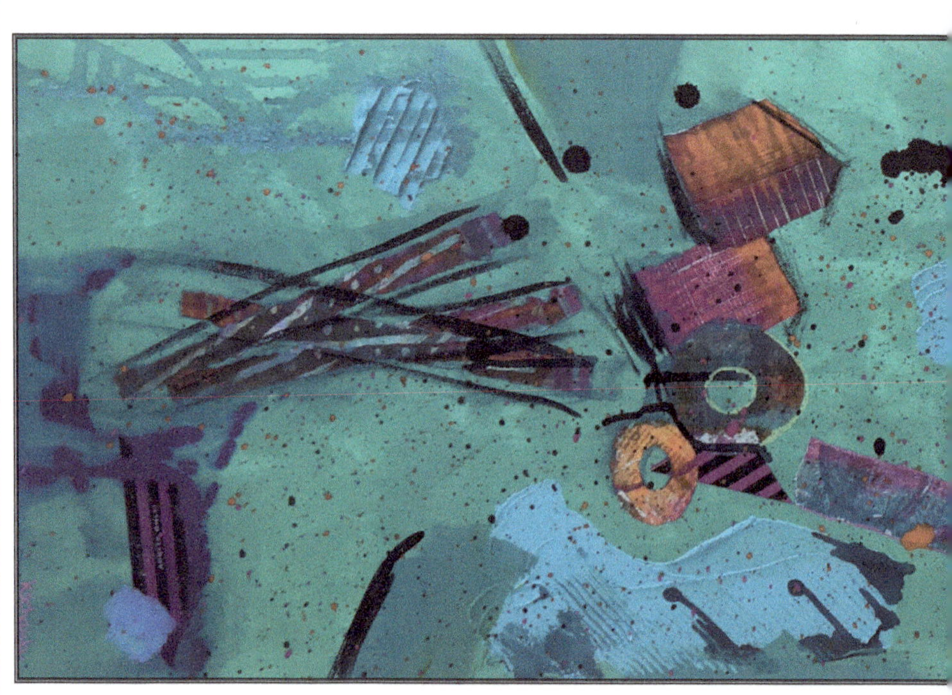

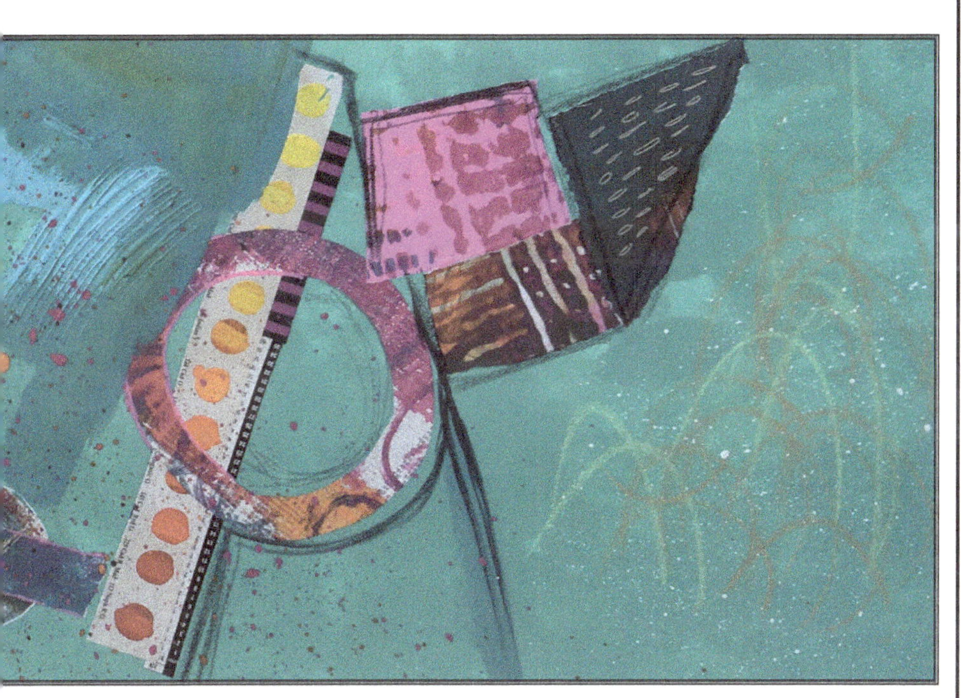

Whatever is Left

Art By Emily Somoskey
Poetry by Martha Kane

72

Leave nothing unbroken
that should not be whole.
Every piece is a piece
unto itself.
Wear holes in the carpet.
Walk forever there.
And look up.
The plasterwork
deserves your notice
and the dangling light
no less than that.
Tear off the paper. Chip at the paint.
Pour out half of the color
In order to understand
what you know is still left.

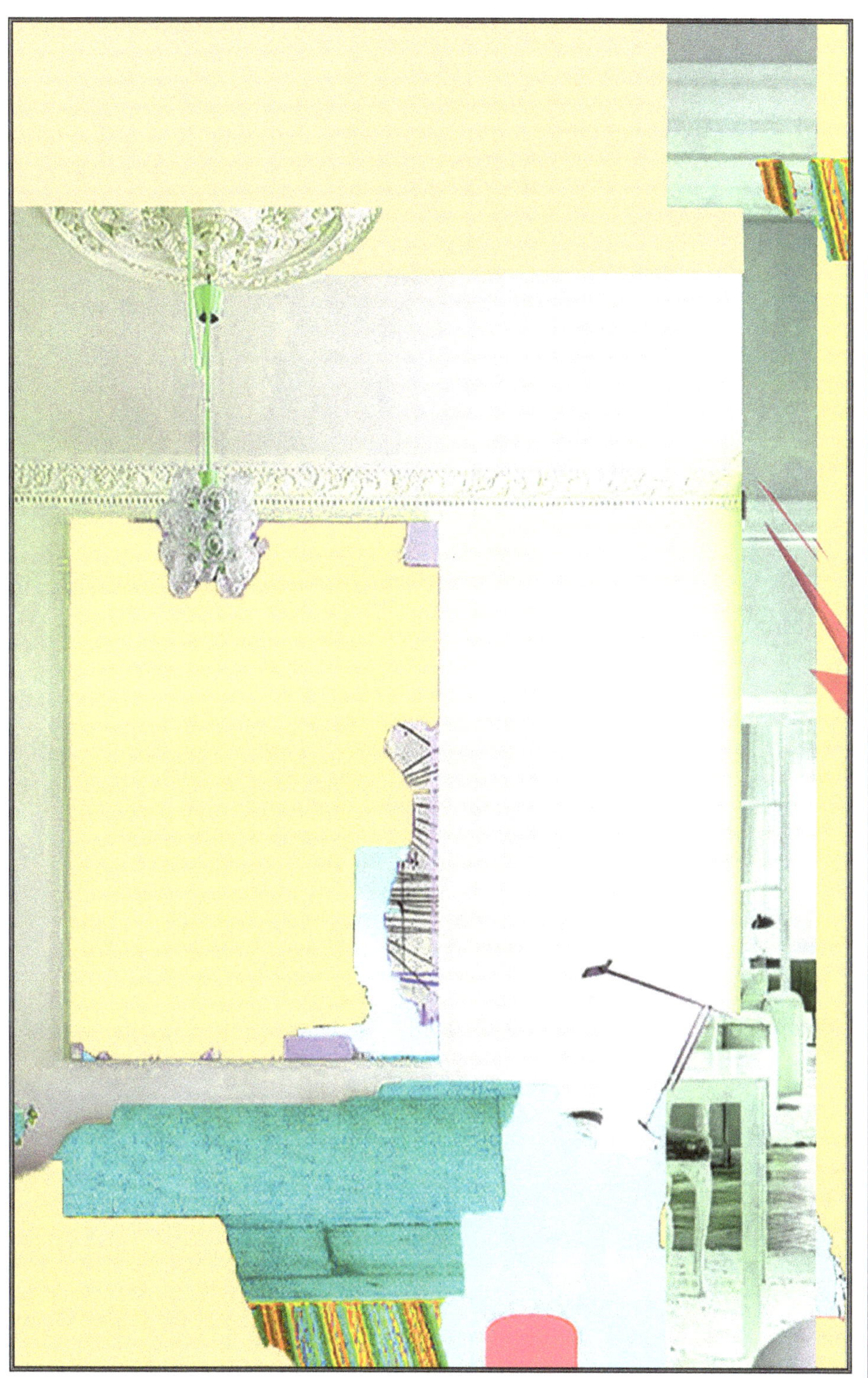

In Order Of Appearance:

M Zaman is allergist/immunologist who lives, with his beautiful wife, in a quaint college town in North Country, NY.His publications include:
1) Poems in thestardustreview.com
2) Epic of Gilgamesh, a Bengali translation of the Sumerian Epic, Published by Anya Prakash, Dgaha, Bangladesh, Feb 2016
3) Life in Light, an English translation of poems by Humayun Kabir; Published by Ghunghur, Dhaka, Bangladesh, Jan 2017
4) Shesh Sraboner Podyo, A Collection of Bengali Poems; Published by Ananya, Dhaka, Bangladesh; May 2007

Nan Williamson is a teacher, artist and author living in Peterborough. She is a graduate of the Humber School for Writers, Toronto, 2013. Her chapbook, leave the door open for the moon, was published by Jackson Creek Press in 2015. Nan is inspired by beauty – natural, or created in art, music, poetry, and secondly, by her love of language and the craft of writing. Her poems have been published in many juried literary journals and anthologies in Canada and the UK. She is the illustrator for Delicate Impact, a Canadian anthology of poetry, A Beret Days Book, The Ontario Poetry Society, 2018. Besides poetry and art, she loves red wine, chocolate, her 1870 home, and Rod's veal stew with black olives.

Savannah based photographer and writer, Briana Gervat, intertwines her passions for storytelling and travel by photographing the ruinous landscapes of history both at home in the United States and abroad in countries that have often known more war than peace. Her love for photography began with the study of American Landscape Painting while obtaining her B.A. in Art History at the University of Mary Washington and she has been traveling, writing, and photographing ever since. Follow her @brianagervat.

Alicja Kusiak-Brownstein is a historian by profession, and native to Poland. She has been living in the U.S. since 2003. A graduate from the University of Michigan, Ann Arbor with Ph.D. in history, she taught for a while at the University of Notre Dame. Currently, she is shifting her career to social services (psychotherapy), studying at the University of Chicago. Her previous publications include scholarly articles, as well as articles in popular press. She published extensively on history, feminism, social issues, and fine arts. She ventures into poetry in search of a new mode of expression.

Katherine Russell is the author of four published books, including a collection of poems on coming of age with cystic fibrosis titled Shapes of Water. Other poems of hers have appeared in Cold Mountain Review and Silver Needle Press. She maintains a blog at www.katherinekeepswriting.com.

Conrad is a Graphic Design student who has won a scholastic silver key in photography (2018) and first place in RAYSAC's media contest (2018). https://kconrad3539.wixsite.com/abby

River E. Hall is a poet, short fiction writer and naturalist. Much of her work focuses on environmental, scientific, and somatic themes. She holds an M.A. in Education and is a graduate of the Wilderness Awareness School's Anake Outdoor program, an intensive nature connection immersion program. She is a wife, a daughter, and a Washingtonian.

Michal Vojtech is a postgraduate student of UCL, UK. Creative writing course at Oxford University for continuing education 2019.

Kathleen Tryon is a Clinical Social Worker and Writer living in Upstate NY. She is a graduate of the Syracuse Downtown Writers Center Pro Program in creative nonfiction and a regular attendant of their poetry workshops. Her work has been published in Sweet, The Stone Canoe, Crab Creek Review, decomP magazinE, and the Readers Write section of The Sun Magazine.

Leah Oates has a B.F.A. from the Rhode Island School of Design and a M.F.A. from The School of the Art Institute of Chicago and is a Fulbright Fellow for graduate study at Edinburgh College of Art in Scotland. In 2019 Oates had work shown in the REVEAL Art Fair in Saratoga Springs, NY with Susan Eley Fine Art and in Toronto 2019 a solo show at Black Cat Artspace and group shows at Propeller Gallery, Xpose 2019 at the Papermill Gallery, Arta Gallery, Neilson Park Creative Centre, Connections Gallery and was part of the 2019 SNAP Photography Auction. Oates has a solo show in spring 2020 at Wychwood Barns Community Gallery in Toronto. In 2018 -2019 Oates had press in Art Toronto, Junto Magazine, Magazine 43, Underexposed Magazine, Ruminate Journal, Mud Season Review, dArt Magazine, The Tulane Review, The Six Hundred JournalBlue Mesa Review, Friends of the Artist, GASHER Journal, Flumes Literary Journal and the 805 Lit + Art Journal. In NYC Oates has had solo shows at Susan Eley Fine Art, The MTA Lightbox Project at 42nd Street, The Arsenal Gallery in Central Park, The Center for Book Arts, Henry Street Settlement and A Taste of Art Gallery and locally at Tomasulo Gallery in New Jersey, Real Art Ways in Connecticut, Sara Nightingale Gallery in Water Mill, Long Island and the Sol Mednick Gallery at at the Philadelphia University of the Arts. Oates has had solo shows nationally at Anchor Graphics, Artemisia Gallery and Woman Made Gallery in Chicago and internationally at Galerie Joella in Turku, Finland.

Mary is a writer living in Houston. She teaches English and Creative Writing to high school students.

Sarah Gane Burton is a freelance writer and copyeditor living in Ooltewah, Tennessee.

Lee Felty is a published artist living in New England, USA. She draws sadness with graphite, then photographs her images - superimposing these images with additional filters to create each piece. What you see is her passion. Her evolution continues.

Nadia Farjami is a seventeen-year-old writer from Southern California. Her work has been featured in The New York Times, Polyphony LIT, Cathexis Northwest Press, Prometheus Dreaming, and more. She's also a two-time National Scholastic Art & Writing Awards Gold and Silver Medalist.

Claire Nelson is a human and poet writing from Savannah, GA. She studied dramatic writing at SCAD with a minor in 3rd person bio writing and earned her creative writing MFA from Florida State University. Currently, she's teaching her dogs how to just take one bite of watermelon.

Holly Woodward is a writer and artist. She lives in Costa Rica with a cat and a dog that came out of the woods. She says, "High Shelf's name reminds her of Emily Dickinson's poem about her 'Silver Shelf:' that begins, It dropped so low--in my Regard.

South Korean artist YIE Ja Min takes a phenomenological approach to observational painting: she captures what is perceived as it arises in the immediate present. The aim is to discard habituated conceptualizations that obscure the natural appearance of things, and so render an expression of "original mind." YIE's work describes reality as luminous and whole; the light of its surface comprises its structural integrity, and intimates the unstained purity of things as they are. YIE received her BFA in Illustration from the Rhode Island School of Design in 2011, and her MFA in Painting from the Marchutz School of Fine Arts in 2017. She has participated in the MASS MOCA Residency Program (2019), Arteles Creative Center SAE Residency (2018), and the Hemera Foundation Tending Space Fellowship (2017). Her works have been exhibited in the US, France, and Canada.

Visual artist Victoria Parker draws inspiration from dream worlds and contrasts in nature and urban environments. She collects odd vintage figurines and beach rocks and is currently saving up dryer lint with which she will make her brother a surprise doll. A native Seattleite, she has also lived in Kalamazoo, New York City and Okinawa, Japan. She lives in Seattle with her husband and two children.

Basmah Sakrani is a Muslim Pakistani-Canadian writer living in Memphis TN with her husband and 2 dogs. Her writing has appeared in Noble Gas Quarterly, Rusted Radishes and won the 2018 Tiferet Writing Contest. She works at Wunderman Thompson and is completing her MFA from Vermont College of Fine Arts. She posts on @BorderlandReflections on Instagram.

Jon Cribb has been working the year as an Instructional Assistant at an elementary school. His educational background is in Creative Writing, where he focused on sentence structure and honing his writing skills. He has written several articles for the Salem Times Register. His biggest accomplishment was turning the Roanoke Review, a literary journal from his alma mater, into a fully online magazine. He has not been published before.

Chris Andrews, who teaches at Western Sydney University, has published two collections of poems – Cut Lunch (Indigo, 2002) and Lime Green Chair (Waywiser, 2012) – as well as translating books of fiction from Spanish and French, including Selva Almada's The Wind that Lays Waste (Graywolf, 2019) and Kaouther Adimi's Our Riches (New Directions, 2020).

Chosen for special recognition by NASA, James Ph. Kotsybar is the first poet to be published to another planet. His haiku currently orbits Mars aboard the MAVEN spacecraft, appears in the mission log of The Hubble Space Telescope, and was featured at NASA's Centaur Art Challenge at IngenuityFest, Ohio. Last Summer, he performed his poetry before an international audience of scientists, journalists and actual Troubadours in their founding city of Toulouse, France, at the EuroScience Open Forum (ESOF2018) by invitation and has been invited back to ESOF2020 to be held in Trieste, Italy. Most recently he has had poems published in The Bubble, Askew, The Society of Classical Poets, LUMMOX Press, Sixfold, Mason's Road, Encore and Scifaikuest, and has received honors from The State Poetry Society of Michigan and the Balticon 48 Poetry Competition. He especially enjoys science poetry, because of its extended shelf-life.

Nathan began his professional life as an actor (originating the role of Jesus in Godspell) but moved into a career as a writer in the late 70s. For over 40 years he has primarily written for film, television and theater winning, among other acknowledgements, the Humanitas Prize, Writers Guild Award, and two Emmy nominations. Nathan has been writing poetry for years and has just decided to start sharing his work. He has recently been featured in Typishly, Cathexis Northwest Press, Paragon Press and Cultural Weekly. Instagram & Twitter @squarechicken

Kelly Schaub is a collage maker and mixed media artist in the quaint coastal community of Rockport, Texas. She loves working with vintage imagery and hand-painted papers. She teaches collage and wants the whole world to give the art of cut-and-paste collage a try! Follow her art on Instagram at @powonwheels

Emily Somoskey is a visual artist and educator from Akron, OH. She attended The University of Akron's Mary Schiller Myers School of Art, in Akron, OH and received a BA in Art Education with a minor in painting in 2013. She is currently a 2nd year MFA candidate at Michigan State University, located in East Lansing, MI. Emily's current work explores the ways we interface with material culture in our everyday lives, specifically the relationships formed between objects and individuals within the constructed domestic living space.

Martha Buffkin Kane has no formal training in poetry. She has been published in many small press magazines many years ago, although she would like to update this history. She lives in Gilford, NH. She writes from wherever she is.

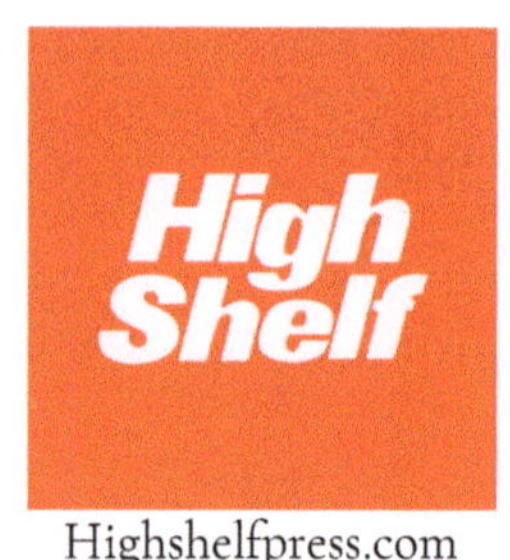

Highshelfpress.com

www.ingramcontent.com/pod-product-compliance
Lightning Source LLC
Chambersburg PA
CBHW050039040726
47599CB00015B/1748